Accidental Patriot

A Diplomat's Journey in Africa

Rediscovering America

Kirsten Bauman

DEDICATION

Thank you to my husband for encouraging me to write
this book and helping me along the way. Thank you to my
kids, for helping me to see the world through your eyes.
Thank you to all our friends in Ethiopia - our support
structure that helped us get through all the ups and downs
together. Thank you to the people of Ethiopia who
touched our lives. Thank you to my sister for your lifetime
of support and my parents for teaching me to aim high
and see where life will take me.

CONTENTS

We the People of the United States, in order to form a more perfect union, establish justice, ensure domestic tranquility, provide for the common defense, promote the general welfare, and secure the blessings of liberty to ourselves and our posterity, do ordain and establish this Constitution for the United States of America.
- Preamble to the U.S. Constitution

"The true genius of America [is] a faith in simple dreams, an insistence on small miracles; that we can tuck in our children at night and know that they are fed and clothed and safe from harm; that we can say what we think, write what we think, without hearing a sudden knock on the door; that we can have an idea and start our own business without paying a bribe; that we can participate in the political process without fear of retribution; and that our votes will be counted." - Barack Obama

"The ultimate determinant in the struggle now going on for the world will not be bombs and rockets but a test of wills and ideas - a trial of spiritual resolve: the values we hold, the beliefs we cherish and the ideals to which we are dedicated." - Ronald Reagan

"One nation. Under God. Indivisible. With liberty and justice for all."

PROLOGUE
A Tale of Two Worlds

"Don't drink and walk in the road. You may die."
— Warning label printed on boxes of wine sold in Addis Ababa,
Ethiopia.

The idea of this book came about one morning during my daily commute to work at the U.S. Embassy in Addis Ababa, Ethiopia. My husband was navigating the dirt roads and paved streets full of potholes that could swallow a truck, dodging buses and taxis intent on running us off the road, and avoiding the pedestrians darting in front of our car on some kind of crazed death wish. He was periodically compelled to stop for the herds of long-horned cows as they crisscrossed the broken streets on their way to the slaughter house, to swerve to avoid single-file lines of donkeys hauling construction materials to Chinese-run building sites, and to slow down when approaching corners where the goats and sheep were aimlessly milling with their vacant stares.

While my husband continued to plod along on our way to the embassy, I absent-mindedly gazed outside our tinted car window in a semi-detached state while listening to the carefree tunes of Jimmy Buffet. Soaking in these chaotic, developing world street scenes from the comfort of our air-conditioned SUV as we slowly meandered through the throngs of animals and people, dodging buses and cows alike, I felt as if I was watching scenes in a movie unfold before me from the comfort of a cushioned theater chair. This cognitive dissonance reached a crescendo when, as the shrimp were beginning to boil in Buffet's Margaritaville, we swerved to avoid hitting a half-naked man laying partially on the median, partially in the street, most likely dead.

It was at that moment that I realized I had a story to tell: the collision of two worlds - American suburbia meets Africa, as told through the eyes of a typical American woman.

The point of this book is not to glorify America or denigrate Africa. Nor is this book meant to be an attack on the international aid machine or a scholarly paper designed to examine the sources of Africa's development woes. Rather, it is simply a compilation of frank observances gathered from an unlikely source. It tells the story of one woman's journey in Africa - while trying to break free of the trappings of her suburban upbringing and simultaneously forced to come to terms with the world's inequities, she happens to rediscover her own country.

I was a typical kid, raised in America's middle class suburbs with a religious adherence to the prescribed suburbanite manual epitomized by the cookie-cutter homes in our cookie-cutter neighborhoods. While my two older sisters thrived in this cloned environment, I never did quite fit in and in time rejected the model altogether.

Seeking my own path in life, I was restless and constantly wandering, living on both coasts of America, in the UK, Czech Republic, Germany, France, Greece, and now Ethiopia. Along the way I completed my studies, I overcame cancer three times over, taught English outside of Prague in the aftermath of the fall of the Berlin Wall, became a diplomat, fell in love, and started a family. All the while, I kept moving, kept searching.

It wasn't until living in Ethiopia - a country drowning under the crushing weight of abject poverty, a nation whose government takes little interest in the meaningful betterment of its own people - that I came to feel an intense amount of respect and pride for my home country.

Witnessing needless suffering in Ethiopia on such a broad scale in a land that lacks opportunity and even hope - a human condition so diametrically opposed to my own experience in life - I found myself continuously torn between emotions of intense guilt for all my advantages in the face of the world's disparities, a crippling sense of responsibility to work for the betterment of the staggering numbers of less fortunate, and an immense wave a gratitude for all the opportunities bestowed upon me and my family simply because of our nationality.

I once had a colleague tell me that as Americans from loving families, we've entered the world having already won the lottery. At the time, while working my first Foreign Service assignment as a U.S. diplomat in Paris, I dismissed his statement as a hollow cliché. It's the type of sentiment that makes Europeans roll their eyes in barely disguised disdain.

Now, however, while living in Africa and witnessing the ravages of poverty and political oppression first hand, I understand what my colleague meant that long-ago day in Paris. Not only have I spent my lifetime taking my inalienable rights for granted, before living in Ethiopia I did not even have the capacity to conceive of what a life without them would be.

It wasn't until viewing the symbolic Presidential inauguration of Barack Obama on a jumbo television in an elegant reception room at Ethiopia's grandest hotel, watching the expressions of the emotional Africans around me as they listened longingly to this embodiment of the American dream speak of human dignity and rights, condemning the corrupt who brutally cling to power at the expense of others, and pledging to work alongside the poor "to nourish starved bodies and feed hungry minds," that I came to truly understand and internalize what it really means to be American. Politics aside, it was profoundly moving to be in a room full of people that fiercely crave these rights; people suffering under the turmoil of political repression and rampant corruption, with their progress stymied and futures suppressed, desperate as they clung to the words of a newly-elected American President for inspiration and hope.

ဆဆၚၚ

I wrote *Accidental Patriot* with a few objectives in mind. It is a frank depiction of life in Africa as told through the true stories of the Ethiopians I've met. Through their stories, I bear witness to their struggles to survive in a tough world where the line between right and wrong is easily skewed, where life is tenuous, and the future unknown. Feeling that their stories deserve to be told, the book describes a world where there are no simple solutions in a complex land dominated by crushing shades of grey. And at the same time, the book highlights the incredible strength of the human spirit to endure.

I also wrote the book as a vehicle to stress what a unique country America is. *Accidental Patriot* pays tribute to the United States and all that the country represents. For the American that knows little of the harsh realities that exist beyond our borders, this book describes what it is like to live without all that we take for granted. For the American financially suffering in the ongoing recession, this book inspires optimism that we are a country of innovation that knows how to adjust, survive, and succeed. For the American disillusioned by our domestic political discourse or our prevailing foreign policy, this book reminds the reader of our enduring core values that bind our nation together and set us apart in the world.

And the book is meant to be inspirational; it is about overcoming obstacles to pursue dreams. This may sound cliché, but when you live in a world void of freedom, opportunity and hope — when you truly experience a place where human life is not universally valued — those seemingly worn clichés take on real meaning. Through this book — in telling the stories of the Ethiopians who have touched my life — I try to bring their world alive to the reader. To enable the reader to experience a life that the vast majority of people on our planet live, so that we can remember to appreciate our blessings. Not only the good life — the luxuries and amenities that we enjoy in the developed world — but rather, the unique qualities of the United States that distinguish us from every other nation on earth. For all our faults, we are a country set apart from all others, a place where people of every color, race, religion and creed are granted the Constitutional right to pursue happiness. If you come to our shores and you work hard, obey the laws, and make positive contributions to society — no matter how small — you are American. We accept you and want you to succeed. It's the American way. The American Dream.

And finally, this book is also the story of my awakening, the story of my quest to find meaning in my experiences in Ethiopia. It is the story of my unexpected journey rediscovering home. As a U.S. diplomat of 14 years, it took these three years living in Ethiopia for me to internalize what it really means to be American — to be from a country that values and honors equality, meritocracy, and individual human worth.

I hope this message will resonate with a U.S. electorate — Democrats and Republicans alike — who are increasingly disillusioned by a degenerating political discourse. In a time of waning national confidence — with the U.S. mired in economic malaise, ongoing wars, and a disappointing domestic political dialogue — I hope that *Accidental Patriot* can serve as a reminder to Americans that we have built something too valuable and too precious to degrade through acerbic political rhetoric and petty squabbling defined by color-coded red and blue camps.

America represents a place of dreams for people the world over seeking an example of a better way of life. It is a place of hope and dreams, where the individual is valued and free. And that means something.

CHAPTER 1

The Party – Farewell to Purgatorial Eden

"In a country well governed, poverty is something to be ashamed of. In a country badly governed, wealth is something to be ashamed of."
- Confucius

How do you define the good life? A basic answer would be secure access to food, clothing, and shelter. Some might add in security from harm and possibly the reasonable assurance of good health. Americans emphasize the notion of liberty and the ability to pursue happiness. I would add to the mix the opportunity to nurture a happy, healthy family, to whom you can provide every possible advantage. My husband says the good life is attained when you have a full cellar of expensive wine and drive a Ferrari.

Perhaps the true definition of the good life is the ability to dream, to aim high and see how far life will actually take you. But for many, success may just be the chance to get by, the ability to survive another day.

ഇഇരുരു

Today is May 31ˢᵗ, the end of the month. How do these days sneak up on me like this? I have to remember to cash a check at the bank today so that I can pay my household staff. There's my indispensable nanny, the housekeeper-cook who also does the grocery shopping, the gardener who doubles as a guard and driveway gate opener, and the driver whose sole job it is to pick my two toddlers up from their expensive preschool every afternoon. I also have to remember to leave money for the children's weekly French class and organize our Saturday with friends at the exclusive Sheraton pool resort where our family has a membership. All this to do before my Sunday work trip to Mauritius and the Seychelles.

I'm checking these tasks off my mental list as I write the day's instructions for the household staff: lunches and dinner to prepare for the kids; do the laundry and wash all five bedrooms' sheets; this is the week for cleaning the rugs including those in the office, library, and workout room; cut the grass and prune the roses that line the full perimeter of our extensive property; and don't bother with dinner because my husband and I will be eating at a reception, so please put the children to bed for us after their dinner and bath.

Not bad for a mid-level U.S. government bureaucrat. But there's a catch. I live in Africa. And it is a place where all these luxuries are negated by the ominous shadows cast by Ethiopia's dark side. I live in a place where deformed beggars drag their gnarled bodies through the dirt and mud and smog in hopes of reaching a sympathetic passerby to receive some small handout; where the blind stumble along the chaotic streets to tap on windows of cars stopped in traffic; and where bedraggled, emaciated mothers carrying babies with vacant eyes wander the city in a desperate search for food or money. These are the faces of extreme poverty that help form the fabric of life in the capital city of Ethiopia, of life in much of Africa, of life in a poor country. And they are the other side of luxury that live just outside my beautiful home's walled enclosure.

Living in Ethiopia, a place where the cost of a manicure could help clothe some of the many children that wander the streets in rags and the bill at a restaurant catering to foreign palates could feed untold numbers of the city's hungry, feelings of injustice taint those every day activities that used to seem mundane. I am constantly blindsided by the vast divide that separates my two worlds. Like when I was watching a CNN report on television in the Nairobi airport in Kenya one afternoon while waiting to catch a delayed airplane back to Ethiopia. Sitting in the stifling hot, non-ventilated waiting room as I swatted away random flies, I listened to the CNN reporter who was talking about the international economic downturn and its subsequent effect on the world fashion industry. In an interview with a fashion designer, this designer offered the following advice to her financially distressed clientele, "If you find that you only have $20 to spend, buy a lipstick. It will keep that smile on your face looking radiant while you wade through these trying times." I had just finished an afternoon viewing the horrors of Nairobi's notorious slums.

It is against this backdrop that I now live with my family in Africa, precariously straddling this line between excess and want as I try to reconcile the privileged existence I enjoy with a very different world struggling on the other side of my home's massive fence.

But don't be mistaken about what brought me to Africa. I am not a missionary. I never joined the Peace Corps or focused on African studies in school. I don't work for a "do-gooder" non-government organization nor am I a war reporter or adventure junkie of any kind. In fact, my worst roughing it experiences took place during the rustic cross-country camping trips of my youth. I'm your typical blond-haired, blue-eyed, white-Anglo-Saxon-Protestant from suburban America who could happily spend a lifetime subsisting off cheeseburgers on sesame seed buns. Yet I somehow woke up one day to find myself a U.S. diplomat married to a political-security analyst, trying to raise my two toddler daughters in Africa with some semblance of normalcy.

My name is Kirsten Bauman and I grew up in the suburbs of Washington, DC, with all the requisite accoutrements of the good, suburban life - a cookie cutter, two-story brick home with a white picket fence for the dog; a station wagon to haul groceries and transport kids to and from soccer, basketball, and softball practice; piano lessons once a week; and so on.

My father was a banker and my mother was a school teacher. My dad grew up in a small town in Pennsylvania, and before going to business school, he had a brief stint in the military after having been drafted for the Korean War. The war ended before he finished basic training, so he used the GI bill to finish school. My mother grew up in a small town in the middle of Ohio. Both moved to big city of Wilmington, Delaware after getting their degrees – my dad to make his mark in the business world and my mother to land herself a husband who was going to make his mark in the business world. They met, married after relentless pressure from my mother, and had three children. All girls.

In my family, the annual, summer cross-country camping trip was a sacred ritual. These Wallyworld-esque vacations consisted of my parents loading my two older sisters and me into our trusty station wagon with the fake wood side panels and driving across the United States until reaching our National Park destination of choice and pitching an old military tent. My mother and middle sister, Jenny, preferred to sleep in the car, leaving my oldest sister, my dad, and me free to stay up late telling ghost stories and making spooky faces using the flashlight. I was always scared, but too timid to admit it and too ashamed to suggest joining the "girlie" people who chose to sleep in the car. The number one rule was to impress dad by being tough and by playing sports; never mind the fact that I was a skinny, gawky beanpole, painfully shy, and grossly uncoordinated.

As my two older sisters and I grew old enough to play on organized sports teams, my dad was intent on putting aside his disappointment with no sons and instead began molding his daughters into strong little athletes. Not only did he sign my sisters and me up for all sports, he also volunteered to be our basketball coach – year, after year, after year. In the process, I unwittingly became the family joke.

It all started on the first play of my very first game as I stole the ball from my opponent. This was good. But while dribbling down the court, I chose this perfect moment to expose my secret-weapon surprise, a glorious milestone I had been keeping to myself for just such an occasion. I could skip! The time was ripe for my debut and off I skipped all the way down the court on my very first fast break. Reaching the basket, I jumped high into the air, basking in my spectacular moment of triumph. And then I panicked. Down to the ground I came crashing with the ball still held tightly in my grasp. There was a collective sigh of pity from the parents watching in the stands. The referee blew his whistle and everyone waited. Amid bemused faces and muffled chuckles, my dad was forced to call time out, come onto the court, and pry the ball from my hands.

Back at the home front, for our meals, we would gather around the circular picnic table that served as our kitchen table. Sitting there, at this converted picnic table painted green, yellow, and white, in the wallpapered room with brown appliances and a linoleum floor, my mother of German heritage would serve dinners such as meatloaf, hotdogs, boiled chicken, ravioli from a can, salisbury steak TV dinners, or one of our favorites – something we called 'stringy meat.' In my family, CheeseWiz was considered a strong cheese and McDonalds reigned supreme.

We are about as white bread as they come. For us, life was good. Life was easy. And life was bland. As I grew up firmly within the clutches of this complacent vanilla world,

I increasingly lamented being a hopelessly trapped outsider condemned to my suburban wasteland.

Unlike me, my two sisters have always been very well-adjusted suburbanites. They are both dutifully carrying the baton and living the good life, the American dream personified. Liz lives in Arizona with her husband and they have twin sons. They both proudly serve in the military. Jenny lives outside of Boston, working in the Information Technology industry with her husband and little girl and making a ton of money. They all live in the suburbs with the requisite accoutrements of the good life - cookie cutter, two-story brick homes with white picket fences for the dogs; big SUVs to haul groceries and transport kids to and from soccer, basketball, and softball practice; piano lessons once a week; and so on.

But not me. I managed to break free with the help of a double-edged sword, otherwise known as Africa.

కొకొ౮౮

My husband Brian and I chose to move to Ethiopia out of a long list of possibilities. As a U.S. diplomat, you sign an oath for worldwide availability based on the needs of service. These needs had led me to Paris, France; Washington, DC; and Athens, Greece and it was now time to move to a hardship assignment. We weighed our options very carefully, and, after extensive research, we deemed Ethiopia to be the best compromise - meeting both needs of service and needs of family. With a deep breath, I declared myself ready for our Africa adventure. I was ready.

Or so I thought.

The problem: Growing up in a typical American middle class household, the amenities I now have access to while living in Africa are unlike anything I could hope to acquire in the United States – clearly, I am living well. Yet sitting in the yard of my beautiful two-story Ethiopian home tended by my mini-army of household staff while sipping a gin and tonic and browsing the latest copy of *Architectural Digest* under a warm December sun, watching the nearby slaughterhouse vultures soar above my house while listening to the crack of a child shepherd's whip just outside my gate, the ruthlessness of humanity sneaks up and slaps me in the face with a frank and shocking boldness.

The sensation is like looking out to sea as the sun begins to set. Brilliant shades of yellow, red, pink, and orange lighting up the sky in an explosion of vibrant color fire, creating an out of body experience as you ponder the wonders that lie beyond that brilliant, distant horizon. And while looking up at this magnificent sky, musing over the beauty and wonder of nature and man's place in this world, a seagull poops on your face. Right smack in the eye, its foul odor shooting straight up your nostrils as you struggle to wipe away the pasty grey goo. It's the inescapable Yin and the Yang of life sucker punching you in the stomach. On a daily basis. Taunting you to find a way to make it stop.

But I can't think like this now. My guests will be arriving soon. After three years, I will soon be leaving this complex place of extremes, and I've set aside today as the day to celebrate - to say goodbye, thank you, and good luck to the Ethiopians who have touched my life. Today, for these special people, I have to find a way to remain positive. I must appear happy. For Fasika alone, I will pretend.

Fasika is my children's nanny and my rock – the person I have consistently relied on to help me adjust to life in Ethiopia. Our housekeeper Tigist and her "adopted" daughter will also be coming to the party, along with my gardener/house guard Shibru, Tesfaye the optimist, my Ethiopian colleague at the Embassy Mesfin, and my driver Getahun.

Thinking over the day's guest list, I stare at my house's security gate topped with razor wire and broken glass, awaiting the arrival of these people with mixed emotions. My mind wanders over my Ethiopian guests' lives – their obstacles and challenges, their uncertain futures. I want to hope the best for them, but I know better. They reside in a tough and capricious world, where everything is fleeting. Unlike me, they can't just walk away, leave it all behind, close the door and turn a corner, starting off into the next phase of life. For my guests, they are trapped. And for them, life is not good. Life is not easy. And life is never bland.

As I start lapsing into this all-too-familiar state of melancholy, a knock at my gate saves me from my thoughts. I paste on my best smile and resolutely walk down the length of my gravel driveway to open the massive metal gate door and greet the day's first arrival. It's Fasika. She has arrived a few hours early to help me prepare. In an instant of seeing her there at my threshold, I know that she is wearing my same forced smile. Perhaps women the world over all own that same look – putting on the best face to mask the turmoil that lurks just below the surface.

CHAPTER 2

Fasika – I Do?

"Love and compassion are necessities, not luxuries. Without them, humanity cannot survive." - *The Dalai Lama*

Marriage is bliss. It's the culmination of the search for a soul mate, of finding that special someone who completes you. A companion for life. That is, if you live in a Hollywood chick flick. For those of us in the real world, marriage is work. But we're apparently hard wired to pursue marriage and really don't stand a chance against its relentless biological forces. And so, we go about our lives, accepting the imperative to one day forgo singlehood, independence, and freedom, making the best of our pre-ordained fate. Yet before we know it, we are so closely linked and entwined in our marriage that we simply can't imagine life without our beloved spouse. Relationship through mutual dependency. Not the best title for the next blockbuster RomCom, but still, it beats the life of a wife in Ethiopia.

Fasika is my children's nanny. She's not your typical Ethiopian woman. Far from meek or demure, Fasika has a fierceness to her that is both inspiring and intimidating. Living in an environment where women are expected to earn the household income while also being held in virtual servitude to all household chores and responsible for the children, it is refreshing to know a woman here that won't allow herself to be pushed around.

Fasika is 29 years old and single, with no intention of giving up her independence. She's a bit of a mystery, periodically dispensing small clues that when pieced together help explain her unusual temperament. The first piece of the puzzle comes when I mention that I am to travel to Djibouti over the weekend for my work.

"Djibouti! That is where my boyfriend lives."

"Really? I didn't know you have a boyfriend. You must miss him."

"No. He is a bad one. He is married now. I think of him like this," she says with a dismissive wave of her hand. But I am intrigued.

"He's married?"

"Yes, she lives here. In Addis. Sometimes she calls me, or I see her in the street. She wants me to come to her for coffee, but I say no." Again the hand gesture. "I think she will kill me. She is bad."

"You think his wife will kill you?"

"Yes, with the poison. Very bad, that one."

Not knowing what to say, I am ready to drop the conversation altogether, but Fasika continues. "I always fight with my boyfriend. Yelling and argue. I'm tired. So I leave. I go to Dubai. My friend is there and she gets me job in a house."

"You just left for Dubai?"

"My daddy cry. He tell me do not go. To stay and marry. He threaten me. He says I end up prostitute or slave. I say no. I don't care. I go."

I'm shocked. Ethiopia is an ardent patriarchal society. A daughter who disobeys her father is unheard of in this culture.

"And so, your boyfriend married another girl?"

"No, he come to Dubai."

"You mean he moved there with you?" Now I'm astounded, my mouth left hanging wide open in surprise. Here, women follow men, not the other way around.

"No. He come to take me back. For Ethiopia. We fight and he beats me, but I stay. My sister calls later, maybe two years, and he is married. The girl is with his baby. But she is always jealous because he wants me. They are bad ones. I forget them now."

Over the course of a few more conversations, I learn that Fasika stayed in Dubai for five years. Despite the persistent objections from her father, Fasika held firm. Eventually, though, nostalgia for her homeland won sway and she made arrangements to return. Although rare for a father to forgive such insolence, Fasika's dad was so happy to have his favorite daughter home in Ethiopia that he accepted her back into the family fold.

It was then that Fasika came into our lives as our nanny, helping to care for our kids, to clean the house, wash the clothes, and basically run our lives. Her tireless work ethic is exemplary, with an initiative and attention to detail that sets her apart. That is, until one week when she became unusually distracted. Putting coveted potable water ice cubes in the refrigerator, the kids' shoes in my pajama dresser drawer, and a ketchup bottle in the shower shampoo holder - something was definitely up.

"Fasika, is something wrong?"

"Nothing wrong."

"Hmm. It's just that it seems like maybe you're upset about something. I just found some books in the cupboard with the dishes."

"I live in apartment now."

"What?"

"My father find me husband."

"What? Are you married?"

"No! I say no. I do not like this man."

"And your father?"

"He is very angry. My family is very angry. They tell me to marry."

"Why?"

"Because my father wants my baby before he dies."

"But your sister had three babies in three years. Isn't that enough?" Fasika's sister is Ethiopian Orthodox Christian and very religious. Her priest says that birth control is bad.

"No, because I am the favorite. I have the face like my daddy's mommy. He wants to see this face on my baby."

"But doesn't he want to see your face happy?"

"He wants to see the baby," is her stone-faced reply.

Fasika resisted her entire family and eventually was forced to move out of the family home. A pariah. A single woman, living alone, shunned by her entire family and disowned by her father is not an enviable life in Ethiopia. Family is everything. And necessary. Living on the brink of poverty, you never know when you may need your family safety net. Fasika has a half-sister who learned this the hard way.

Dying of cancer, dismissed by her family and ignored by her husband, Fasika's half-sister Salem is alone and scared. But it is her fate. She married a man despite the father's objections and moved outside of Addis Ababa and away from her father and family to live with the new husband. At that point, she was dead to the family. The fact that her husband turned out to be a drunk who regularly beats her, and that she is destitute in a desperately poor country, is no matter. When Fasika's family learned of the shunned half-sister's terminal sickness and intense suffering, the father said Salem died many years ago and refuses to visit or help.

In this context, Fasika's decision to refuse her father's choice of husband and to move out of the family home is no trivial matter.

"Well, do you like your apartment?" I ask, not really knowing what to say.

"Yes! I have a shower just like you!" she exclaims, her face beaming with pride. But then she turns serious again. "I miss my family. The man is good man. But I do not want him. He is very old." Her voice trails off to near silence at the end of her sentence. It is obvious that she is in agony. "You think I do the good thing?" she almost begs of me.

"Fasika, I don't know. You're an incredibly strong and brave woman. You know what is best for you. For me, I know marriage is hard, and being a mom is even harder. I can't imagine being married to someone I didn't love."

But is love an option here, I think to myself as I look into Fasika's desperate, imploring eyes. Perhaps my thoughts are too transparent. Fasika buries her face in her hands and runs out of the room.

Weeks go by, with random items showing up in strange places in the house. Like my husband's underwear in my closet. Obviously, life is still in upheaval in Fasika world.

ⅫⅫⅬⅬ

"I went to the movies," Fasika announces to me one evening as I am helping to make dinner, a mischievous grin spanning the full length of her face.

Something is obviously amiss. Fasika has consistently made an ingratiating point of saying she never goes out. She's not interested. Only work.

"What did you see?"

"It was Ethiopia movie. It was a date." Her growing smile exposes a mouthful of gleaming white teeth that radiate the room.

"A date?! Who is the man?"

"He is my friend. He is my good friend a long time ago. But he asked me to marry him. I say no and he not talk to me anymore. Now, I see him again after many years and he takes me to the movie."

"I'm so happy, Fasika! You look happy too."

"He says I must marry him. I can tell him my answer in two weeks." The smile begins to dissipate.

"Huh? You just see him after many years and he gives you two weeks?"

"This is how it works. He is better than the other one. He was my friend. Maybe this is the best way. But I don't know." At this point, her playful smile is gone.

"Do you think you could be happy with him?"

"My father must be happy. I think my friend is good man. Everyone says he is a good man. But you never can know. The men can change. Only God knows. It is for God." She looks up and waves her hands in the air.

Well, it looks like two more weeks of ketchup in the shower, I think to myself as I ponder the impressive fact that Fasika has somehow managed, though sheer force of will and fierce determination, to beat the odds of her culture's crushing expectations. That is, until now. But maybe she'll find a way out.

A few more days pass.

"Will you visit my apartment? I got the furniture."

"Sure, Fasika. I'd love to. Does that mean no marriage?" I ask, almost relieved that she's standing her ground.

"I don't know."

And so the wait continues. Given the lack of news as the days tick away, it looks like Fasika may actually manage to stand firm and defy her father for a second time. Maybe.

ಔಔೞೞ

The two-week deadline comes and goes with no news from Fasika. I'm reluctant to ask, to intrude or influence, so I go about my daily business, a creature of routine. Stumbling out of bed, my first morning task is to fumble my way downstairs for a strong pot of heavenly Ethiopian coffee. No day can start until that elixir has entered my system.

It's a Tuesday in May at 6:30am. I say hello to Fasika in the kitchen as I pour my coffee into my large, welcoming mug that has U.S. Embassy Paris emblazoned across the front. Paris – my first diplomatic assignment as a single, young woman with no children seems like eons ago. Another lifetime, I silently muse as I descend into the depths of a drowsy, nostalgic daydream full of buttery croissants and leisurely strolls down the *Avenue des Champs-Élysées.*

"Will you come to my wedding?" Fasika asks, wrenching me from my happy thoughts. So unexpected, and way too early in the morning for an ambush, I nearly spit out my mouthful of hot coffee at her. Not knowing how to respond, I manage to recover quickly enough and reach out to give her a hug.

"Of course I will! Congratulations. I'm sure it's the right decision and you'll be very happy."

She flashes a nervous smile. "I hope. God knows."

"When is the wedding?"

"This weekend."

ೞೞೞೞ

And so it happened. Just like that, Fasika is married. Her fierceness diminishes daily as she slowly slips away into a drone-like state of a beaten-down Ethiopian wife. Just two weeks after the wedding, when my husband - using his most chipper voice - asked her how married life was treating her, she replied matter-of-factly with a tone best described as bitter contempt, "I clean his house."

No blushing bride, no fairy princess dreams coming true with a knight in shining armor, no bliss. No Hollywood script in the making.

For Fasika, marriage is not the culmination of the search for a soul mate, of finding that special someone that completes you. It is not having a companion for life or even the attainment of relationship through mutual dependency.

Love does not appear to be an option for many in Ethiopia. Only work. And that's that.

CHAPTER 3

The Party – The Night Before, No Problem

It's Friday evening. My husband and I just got home from the embassy. I have only one more week of work - I'm leaving Ethiopia next Saturday night. Our house is virtually empty, everything having been packed up and shipped out two weeks ago. The only big thing left to do is to throw a goodbye party for my Ethiopian staff and friends.

"Brian, did you call the café and reconfirm that they have our order and will have all the food ready for pick up tomorrow by 11am?" I try to sound nonchalant, but this food order has me very nervous. If there's a screw up with the food, I'm in big trouble.

"Oops. I forgot."

"What?!" My face muscles start to twitch. "How could you forget?! I told you three times today. Three times!"

"Chill. I'll call them now," he grumbles as he walks away to get his cell phone.

I had ordered a massive amount of Ethiopian food from a local place that Fasika recommended. Brian and I stopped by the restaurant to place the order one week ago, with Fasika's list of dishes written out in Amharic, but unfortunately we did not leave the place with confidence.

The café turned out to be one of the many small shacks with a tin roof, cracked plastic chairs, and wobbling tables covered with dinghy table cloths.

When we walked inside this particular empty café, adjusting our sight to the dim interior, we eventually noticed a woman sitting in the back corner near the counter. We approached her and said hello. She ignored us, staring blankly at a cigarette hole burned into the tattered table cloth in front of her. I bent down closer to her and said hello again, in both English and Amharic. At a painfully slow pace, she raised up her head, looked at us in the same way she had been gazing at the cigarette burn, and then slowly made her way behind the counter.

Having exhausted my knowledge of Amharic with my hello greeting, I just handed her my note from Fasika. Fasika had listed the food that I should request, the quantity, and the date and time for pickup. It was quite a substantial order — one that would surely overwhelm this place's small kitchen, but it would also pull in quite a profit. Yet the girl looked neither anxious nor concerned or even happy with our order. Nothing seemed to register.

"Is ok?" I asked, pointing to the note, imploring her to acknowledge at least our existence, if not the massive order of injera, dora wat, shiro, and many other traditional Ethiopian dishes.

"Ok."

I continued to stare at her. I needed more reassurance.

"Is ok." She repeated. "No problem."

Oh no. There it was. In Africa, anytime someone says no problem, it's a problem. Knowing my intense dislike of this seemingly innocuous phrase, and seeing my fists begin to clench and unclench, Brian quickly ushered me out of the café, saying thank you in Amharic over his shoulder as he pushed me through the doorway.

Left standing on the sidewalk just outside the café, I was at a loss. "I'm throwing a party for a large group of Ethiopians and I need food. I could never come close to being able to cook these complicated Ethiopian dishes. So, what am I supposed to do? I have no options but to rely on someone to make the food. It shouldn't be this hard!"

"Hey, calm, calm. It's ok. You're just stressed out about moving." Brian put his hands on both my shoulders and made me look him in the eyes. "It's just food. They'll do it. They have Fasika's request in writing. I'll call them in a couple days and confirm the order, and then I'll have Fasika call. We'll have the food."

"Yeah, just like we had Alexandra's birthday cake. No problem."

A few months ago, Brian had ordered a princess birthday cake from a nearby bakery that had just opened and appeared to cater to foreigners. We were so thrilled that this new bakery had agreed to bake a cake with pink icing and a marzipan princess crown for us that we couldn't help but break the surprise to Alexandra the day before her birthday. It was all she could talk about.

Then, the morning of her party, Brian drove to the bakery to pick up the prized cake at the agreed-upon time. He arrived. No cake. No recollection of the order. No problem.

Brian returned home without a cake to a devastated Alexandra. Weeks afterward, her face still dropped at the memory of that "yucky brown rectangle" brownie cake I threw together at the last minute.

"Come on, get in the car," Brian said, ignoring my comment about Alexandra's cake as he pointed to a smattering of people making their way towards us to ask for money.

That was last week. Today is Friday, tomorrow is the party. And Brian forgot to confirm the food order.

"Do you even have their phone number?"

Brian rolls his eyes and starts to dial. I hear the familiar beep — no network coverage. Our landline telephones virtually never work and the cell phones are spotty at best. The Chinese built Ethiopia's mobile network at a discounted rate.

"Try again," I say just as the lights in our house go out. I hear the kids scream out "generator!" from where they're watching a DVD, and then they start counting. This is one of our family games — to see how high we count until the embassy-provided automatic generator kicks in to bring back the electricity. Tonight, the girls get to six before the lights are back. Pretty slow. Usually it's more like three or four seconds in the dark.

"MOM!" And now the real screaming starts. The DVD needs to be restarted and then fast forwarded to exactly where they had left off before the power cut.

I shoot Brian daggers with my eyes, and I shout "UGHH!" as I leave him to go to the kids, all the while hearing the "no network" beep from his cell phone.

I fix the DVD and stomp back to Brian, barking out orders as I walk "Did you check the backup water tank out back? I don't want to run out of water tomorrow. And don't forget to soak the vegetables I bought yesterday in bleach like I asked. I don't want anyone getting sick. And while you do the veggies, I'll check that the water distiller machine is still working. We can't be without drinkable water — if that machine breaks again, I really am going to lose it."

Ending my rant, I hear Brian mumbling something. "What? What are you saying? Brian, are you even listening to me?!"

Brian hits the end button on his cell phone. "Food will be ready. I just spoke to a man who is the cousin of the owner."

"So?"

"Let me finish. This cousin of the owner is an Ethiopian-American — he lives in Washington, DC but is in Addis visiting family and was at the café when I called. So, I spoke with this fluent English speaker and he assured me the entire order will be ready by 11am tomorrow."

As Brian spoke, I exhaled. I think it was the first time since getting home that evening that I had actually breathed.

"Kirsten, you have to chill. It's just a party. It'll be fine. You'll do the best you can, given the circumstances that you're operating under. Please, breathe."

I started to tear up. Moving time is always emotional, and this move - after three intense years in Ethiopia - tops the scales. "It's just that I want everything to be perfect for all these people that have done so much for us and have so little. I want to give them something they deserve."

"You will."

"But so much is out of my hands, out of my control. Why can't I just use water from the kitchen sink instead of a distiller machine? Why do I have to bleach my vegetables?"

"Because Addis has open sewers and it doesn't treat its water - we don't want to get parasites or cholera."

I keep going despite Brian's interruption. "Why can't I just call Dominoes and order a dozen pizzas to be delivered to my house at noon?"

"Because the phones don't work, roads don't have names, and no one has an address. What would you say even if you got through — turn right at the banana stand and left at the goats?"

I smile. Brian always makes me smile. "Well, it worked for all our friends." The map I made to show people how to get to my house when I first moved here actually does say "go toward the Vatican Embassy and turn right at the banana stand and left at the goats."

"Except that one BBQ party when the goats weren't there and half the guests got lost!" I say and we both laugh at the memory. With that, the tension I had been generating all evening finally starts to evaporate.

"Kirsten," Brian says brushing my hair aside and rubbing my cheek, "Look at me. It will be fine. Everything will be fine."

Yes, with Brian at my side, all will be fine. It always is.

And on this thought, the lights go out again. "Generator! One, two, three, four," the kids shout out again. This time, I smile and give Brian a big hug. My mutually dependent love runs deep.

CHAPTER 4
Brian – You Do!

"I love being married. It's so great to find that one special person you want to annoy for the rest of your life." - Rita Rudner, actress

Spring was in the air. I had just moved to Paris to begin my first assignment in the U.S. Foreign Service as a diplomat. And being a carefree and blissfully happy, young single woman, I was quickly anointed the embassy's unofficial happy hour coordinator. For my first real big event, something beyond a simple after work drink, I decided to arrange a full-blown Saturday dinner and jazz night out-on-the-town extravaganza.

I was nervous about getting everything just right for this big night out so soon after my arrival in this beautiful city, so I did my homework. Having finally made it into the league of sophisticated diplomats, I pulled out the reference book that everyone should use when trying to impress – *Cheap Eats Paris* - and picked a restaurant close to the jazz club. I chose the jazz club because it was a evening hang out of choice with the U.S. Congressional delegations that shuffled through this city every spring and summer.

The name of the restaurant that came highly recommended in *Cheap Eats*, I later discovered, translated to Pig's Foot, the jazz club was an overpriced tourist trap, and I arrived late to the event. But I'm getting ahead of myself.

The day had started like nearly every other Saturday, at my favorite neighborhood café for a *café crème* and *omelette mixed*. But by mid-afternoon, the day had taken an unexpected turn.

The crimp in what otherwise would have been impeccable planning happened when a friend called me on my cell phone to convince me that I absolutely had to take a Salsa dancing lesson with her that very afternoon. Of course, I protested. I told her I had been kicked out of aerobics and yoga classes for extreme lack of coordination and I even feared the thought of entering a spinning class. But nothing I said would convince her that going alone would be better than showing up with me, and before I knew it, I was walking into a dilapidated building's basement across town. This didn't bode well for my upcoming Pig's Foot-jazz night.

The dance studio was located in an abandoned warehouse with a brightly colored makeover that left me with the impression of being inside a clown's minibus. But having recently established itself as a trendy hangout, it was crowded with eager dancers. In Paris, trendy hangouts generally had a lifespan of a couple of months, tops. Hence my friend's urgency in showing up for a lesson that very day.

Having accomplished the most important part of my job as tag-along friend (which means that I had successfully walked through the door with her so that she wouldn't be stigmatized as the person who showed up alone), I very slowly turned to quietly sneak out. But just as I crossed the threshold and could taste my freedom only steps away, a tiny, flamboyant Cuban man jauntily came through the door, grabbed both my wrists, spun me around, and in heavily Cuban-Spanish accented French, said, "Don't tell me my partner is leaving before we start?"

Partner with the instructor? Mortified, I turned a few shades redder than the bright clown paint on the walls. He took pity on me and let me go. Good decision.

Did I mention that I'm a bad dancer? A really bad dancer. I so lack rhythm that I avoid clapping my hands, tapping my feet or even swaying to music. I don't even know how to snap. It's just not pretty. With freestyle dancing so far out of my reach, I was completely dumbfounded by the fact that I had willingly gotten myself in a situation where I was about to be told how and where to place my feet according to some counted beat. Never mind that those instructions were going to be delivered in a heavily-accented Cuban version of French - a language I could barely understand in the best of circumstances. I was doomed.

As the music started and Cuba Guy began calling out his directions, however, I was somehow magically transformed into the epitome of grace. I became inexplicably blessed with the gift of rhythm, my feet taking on a life of their own, moving in perfect unison to the beat. Picture a shining beam of light coming down through the ceiling, illuminating only me, guiding my movements in an elegant display of perfection.

Or picture bumper cars. More fittingly, picture a class full of dancers and an H1 Hummer slamming into them, the worst casualty being the feet of the poor guy that unknowingly was paired with a blond version of Elaine from Seinfeld.

Somehow, though, I managed to survive this humiliating dance experience. Saying my goodbyes and promising never to come back, I had to rush home to get ready for the main event – dinner and jazz. With only enough time for a quick shower, I got ready in record time and made my way to the "chic" *Pied du Couchon* (i.e. Pigs Foot).

𝈔𝈔𝈕𝈕

The Night

I was late. Not ideal, but when I arrived disheveled and winded, I was quick to surmise that at least people had shown up. Everyone in fact, right down to the new guy.

There are a couple of things worth mentioning about my husband-to-be before I continue with this story of how we met. First, he is a lover of good food and wine and takes his restaurant choices very seriously. Second, he worked for Versace just before I met him. Also, he is a voracious reader, buys his books in hard back, and treasures them like precious works of art. Oh, and he loves to dance.

So here I come, bounding in through the restaurant door, spouting off lame apologies and false excuses for being late, and I sit down at the one remaining empty seat which happened to be next to New Guy. Lucky for me - New Guy, it turns out, is very good looking. Tall, blond, tan, hazel eyes, and confident. The sexy kind of confident that draws you in. Not only that, but he is funny, smart, and seemed to be paying an inordinate amount of attention to me. It was all too good to be true - I didn't even realize that the restaurant was a cold and dank dump that served disgusting meat concoctions from swine joints. Something had to go wrong.

A few minutes into my arrival, I warmed up and took off my jacket. But as I looked down at my shirt, I realized with dismay that it was on backwards with the outline of a bulky tag showing. This was trouble. The first thing New Guy said to me when I arrived was that he had worked in fashion and he liked my shoes. That was the second fashion complement I had received in a week, the first being from a French colleague that told me when I had first arrived in Paris a month ago, I dressed like a farmer, but she had noticed I had been getting a little better recently.

With these two complements in tow, I was riding high. And then the shirt. Maybe no one would notice? No, my plan would have to be to quickly run to the bathroom and switch it around before New Guy realized I was "fashion backwards." With that thought, I started to giggle.

"What's so funny?" Theresa asked from across the table.

I glanced over at New Guy who was deep in conversation with the person on his right, something about Israel and the Middle East. Looked safe to let someone in on my problem. I turned the top part of my shirt down to reveal the tag. I expected Theresa's reaction to be a look of pity or even disbelief at how someone could actually be so stupid. Instead, she let out a full-throttle laugh. Every conversation stopped and all eyes were on us. I looked at New Guy with a part guilty, part panic look.

New Guy took in my look and tried to casually ask, "What's the joke?" although by his tone it was clear that he thought we were laughing at him. I had to come clean. Down came the top of the shirt again, with tag in full view for all to see.

"Have you heard the one about the blond who can't dress herself?" I wasn't sure if a dumb bond joke at this moment was the best way to win over my intellectual and sophisticated new crush, but we were eating at the Pig's Foot and my shirt was on backwards.

"I've actually done that before. The thing is, you usually catch it because the stretched part is in the back when it's on backwards." Big-breasted Karen, a few seats down, spoke up in an attempt to show solidarity.

"Wish I could say that would work for me, but these tiny things don't stretch my clothes," I said pointing at my small boobs. At this point I knew I had blown it with New Guy, so why not throw in a token small-chest joke.

Yet somehow, apparently, the evening hadn't been a complete disaster. Not only did New Guy not write me off as a flat-chested, ditzy, pig-foot eating loser, but he actually asked me on a "second date."

Date two rolled around a few days later and I felt the pressure. Our first meeting had been very casual and unexpected. But this time, it was a date. I had to be witty. I had to be interesting. I had to be sophisticated. I could not be goofy. New Guy did not look like he dated goofy. As the evening drew near, the pressure of comporting myself through an entire goofy-less evening became asphyxiating.

It was in this frame of mind that I met New Guy at a little romantic restaurant he had chosen based on its description of phenomenal meals and a quirky décor of teapots. There were teapots everywhere – on the walls, the shelves, the tables, hanging from the ceiling. You couldn't be in that small dining room and avoid the topic of teapots. I arrived on time, sat down and began racking my brain for something interesting to say about teapots. Nothing came, so the rambling began.

Once started, you can't stop a ramble. It moves by the force of its own uncontrollable inertia, particularly the bad rambles. And this one was very bad, with the pained expression on New Guy's face rapidly leading me toward a frenzied-panic ramble. In no time, I had my whole body into it, lurching from side to side, arms flailing. Out of control, the inevitable casualty was eventually sacrificed as I sent my glass of red wine tumbling.

On the one hand, the spilt wine put an end to the ramble, but it also completely saturated a pile of New Guy's just purchased hard back books from the expensive English book store on *Rue Rivoli*. Strike two. A big strike two. But New Guy, an apparent masochist, for some inexplicable reason asked me out on a third date.

For date three we went to another restaurant of his choice and had another amazing meal. This time, the evening progressed without incident and was extremely enjoyable. New Guy was personable. He was easy to talk to and fun company. I could really see myself falling for him and was beside myself. The clichés were nauseating – falling in love in Paris in the springtime. I couldn't help but let my mind wander.

"So, are you up for it?"

"What?" How long had I been daydreaming?

"MonteCristos. It's just up the street. I went a couple of weeks ago – it's fun, not too crowded at this time of night. We don't have to stay late." I was dubious.

He read my expression, so he kept talking. "Listen Kirsten, I just don't want to say goodnight yet. I want to spend more time with you," he added, holding my hands tightly in his as he leaned in to give me our first kiss. I was dazed. He had so dazzled me, I'd follow him anywhere, and off we went.

MonteCristos, it turns out, is a dance club. Strike three. By this time, though, we'd passed the first kiss hurdle so I could now officially distract him with more kissing. By the time we left the club a couple hours later, a sufficient amount of kissing and alcohol had thankfully kept us off the dance floor and I successfully made it to the coveted date four and beyond.

ဆဲဆဲလ်လ်

The Noose Comes Out

Brian Bauman and I continued dating and spent a magical summer discovering Paris together. We would sprawl out in *Parc Monceau* on the weekends after a brunch of *jus d-orange pressé, café crème,* and *omelette mixed* and mouth-watering buttery croissants and he would read Dave Barry's weekly column to me from the *International Herald Tribune.* We would stroll hand-in-hand along the *Champs-Élysées* and duck into hidden side street cafes to sip wine late into the evenings. Renting cars on the weekends, we would plan day trips that would take us meandering through the bucolic French countryside. Bliss wraps it all up perfectly.

But, as if on cue, this is just about the time that things come to an abrupt end according to the Kirsten timeline. My life since leaving my childhood home in Maryland had fallen into a predictable pattern revolving around two-to-four year intervals, and this European segment was no exception. My Paris clock was ticking and I was running out of time.

I decided to play aloof and live in the moment, fully expecting the "it's been great" line to come crashing down on me at each turn. It all left me is a state of suspended terror, both fully alive and increasingly paranoid. With one week left in Paris before moving back to Washington, DC, and still no "talk," after a two minute pause in conversation over a *magret de canard* lunch, I just couldn't take it anymore. Out of the blue, I surprised both Brian and myself by blurting out, "What are you waiting for?"

"What?" His response was nonchalant as he took another sip of wine.

"I'm not stylish."

"What?" I was starting to get his attention.

"I have no talent. I can't even snap my fingers."

"Yeah, that's a deal breaker," he said with a loud, dramatic snap.

"I knew it! I knew you were trying to break up with me."

"What?" I think he was actually smirking. "Because you can't snap?" How could he find humor at such a traumatic moment?

"Just tell me it's over." I was starting to tear up. Here it was. It was finally coming to an end and this time it was really going to hurt. Don't get me wrong, by this time in my life I'd become a pro at the break up scene. And by that I mean I knew how to be dumped. But this was different.

"Kirsten, you don't get it. I love that you can't snap. I love that you wear your shirts backwards and that you dance like Elaine. I even can put up with your snore. I love all your imperfections and want to discover more. I'm not ready to say goodbye."

Hmm. That was unexpected. I was confused and speechless.

"Kirsten, are you ok? You don't look happy."

After a long pause, I closed my eyes and with quiet determination declared, "I don't snore." With that, I walked over to his side of the bistro table, gave him a long, tender kiss and ate the rest of lunch sitting on his lap. You can do that in France.

಄಄ೞೞ

The One?

I had been dating someone before moving to France. We were together for a little over two years and I thought I might be in love. I had even realized that I was ready for marriage over the course of our time together. The question I grappled with was whether I was ready to marry him.

This is the eternal question. How do you know when he's "the one?" I embarked on a research campaign, asking my parents, their friends, my married friends, their parents, acquaintances, basically anyone who would talk to me. And when you ask a woman this question, she'll talk. It should be the opener in any interrogation. I discovered that women just can't resist the opportunity to describe their moment when they "just knew."

Some said the revelation came when they realized they couldn't picture their life without this person by their side. Others said they knew they wanted this person's children. Yet another common response was they were so comfortable in this person's company that they could fully enjoy being in their vicinity without the need to talk. Some even used the worn cliché "it was obvious we were soul mates" or "it was simply love at first sight."

As I listened to the litany of these Hollywood-inspired recaps, I couldn't help but be skeptical. It seemed like the explanations were concocted with the benefit of hindsight - that the story existed precisely because the relationship had ended in marriage. That said, I ended my research with the decision that I would marry my boyfriend. I had no intention of pressuring him, but would wait for the inevitable and then say yes. My reason? I shared the emotions of all the above mentioned explanations, so having checked all the boxes, I decided there was no reason not to marry him.

A few days after reaching this "revelation," the inevitable came from my boyfriend – not in the form of a proposal, but as a "talk." The break up caught me completely by surprise, but I somehow found it shockingly easy to absorb. Maybe it was because I was heading off to Paris to be a U.S. diplomat and nothing, not even a dump, could dampen my spirits. Besides, in retrospect, this break up had saved me from having to tell future generations that the story that the reason I had married my husband was because I had no reason not to.

With Brian, Mr. New Guy Masochist, it was all different, from the ease of our days together in Paris, to the seamless transition into long distance dating. I never went through that soul searching period with Brian that I had with the other one – one day I really did just know.

It happened after returning home to Washington, DC after a routine visit with boyfriend Brian in Paris. Walking into my quiet, lonely two-room basement apartment in Georgetown after another amazing visit with Brian in Paris, I looked at a framed picture sitting casually on my kitchen counter of Brian and me together on vacation in Istanbul, our obliviously happy expressions almost illuminating the picture itself, I suddenly knew that Brian was "the one." I dropped my suitcase in the little corner space next to my two-room basement apartment door, picked up the phone mounted on the kitchenette wall, and called him immediately.

$\mathcal{EOEOCSCS}$

And the Noose Tightens

"Hi honey. You have to marry me."

"What?" That seemed to be his recurring response to me.

"I just wanted you to know that what we're doing is going to end in marriage. It has to. It's only fair that you should know that."

"What time is it?" Poor guy. Not only had I completely blindsided him, I did it in the middle of the night Paris time.

"Just tell me that you're not opposed to the idea of marriage to me. That's enough for now. If you're still figuring things out, or you're just enjoying this long distance thing until you don't anymore, that's unacceptable."

"What's gotten in to you? It's three in the morning. Is something wrong?" I think he was starting to wake up now.

"No, no. I'm fine. I'm great and perfect. Happiest ever. We're going to have a great life together. I want to run and sing and shout."

"Just don't dance."

"No, I'm so happy, I even want to dance," I said with exuberance. I had the energy of someone who has discovered the key to happiness, the reason, the one.

"Ok, you dance. I'll sleep. Let's talk later," he said in the most pathetic, groggy voice he could muster.

"We'll talk later and forever. I love you."

And with that, a pressure campaign commenced that would make my mom proud. Every phone conversation, every email, every visit was replete with references to our life together, forever.

The fact that he humored me rather than dumping me at this stage was a good sign - my insane tenacity was very annoying. But not only did he not dump me, at one point in the middle of one of our typical daily phone calls, he off-handedly said that he "loved me madly." I was stunned and made him repeat the phrase several times. Poor guy thought he had done something really wrong.

The thing is, I'm a quiet, low key, unassuming, completely forgettable, recovering nerd. I do not inspire "madness." Boredom, yes. Interest, maybe. Madness, no way. But he said it, and he actually meant it. I hadn't been fishing nor had he been coached in advance. This man was definitely for me and his madly comment sank the final nail into his coffin.

ജ്ഞ്ജ്ഞ്ഞ്ഞ്ഞ്

That Magic Moment

While the good-natured banter concerning our future pleasantly continued, time passed and there was still no ring in the picture. I was starting to get nervous. I would sit down with friends and colleagues just before each work trip that took me from my home in Washington, DC to or through Paris and declare that this visit would be the one – that he most definitely was going to propose. Yet I always came back empty handed. Literally. Time and time again I'd go off on long trips to places like Uzbekistan, Vietnam, and Dubai and return without a ring. I began to read pity in peoples' eyes and had suspicions that some were beginning to doubt the whole "boyfriend in Paris" story altogether.

Things were dire and my pressure had reached frenetic proportions. Brian continued to go along with all my demands, but no proposal. Then, one day, I got a call from my sister Jenny in Massachusetts. Jenny is thirteen months older than I to the day. She is Jenny the Beautiful, Jenny the Blessed with a Midas touch.

And Jenny's news? Her boyfriend who she had been dating for a year had just proposed. He had measured her ring finger with a piece of string while she slept, did the research, and purchased a stunning ring. He then booked a bed and breakfast at the Cape and took her there saying they had to attend a family reunion, but surprised her with a proposal.

Now that's the story I wanted. I was obsessed with the fact that Brian was my "one." But with all this conviction, I could not bring myself to interfere with what in my school-girl fantasy mind was to be a magical, surprise engagement. I never bought into the Hollywood image of love at first sight, had no interest in a wedding, but absolutely wanted that engagement moment. So I waited. I pressured him and waited. The trips to Paris continued to come and go. The tension on the last days of each of my visits was palpable, but still no ring.

What kept me going was the fact that we had planned a two-week trip to Florida in the coming months. We had planned to stay a few days in South Beach and then rent a convertible and drive to Sanibel Island and then Key West. Surely, he was planning to get on his knee at some point during this trip. With this end in sight, I could put up with a little more waiting.

Our days in South Beach came and went. We moved on to Sanibel, a beautiful, natural setting where we spent long hours strolling along the stunning beach and taking nature walks in the pristine setting. Nothing. But Key West, with its mesmerizing sunsets, was just over the horizon. That had to be the place – land of Jimmy Buffet, margaritas, key lime pie, and world renowned sunsets.

Nope. After our last island sunset, I silently cried myself to sleep. The next morning, we loaded up the convertible and drove back to Miami. I said a total of maybe five words to him during the entire drive. As we pulled into the car rental return at the Miami airport, he turned to me to ask if everything was ok, that I seemed just a little too quiet.

With that entry, I exploded. I had been seething for hours and immediately launched straight into a tirade. Things like "how dare you think you can lead me on like this" and "I'm fed up with your games and false sentiments" and "you should be ashamed and lucky that I'm not slapping you across the face for everything you've put me through" came flying out of my mouth.

He was stunned. He later told me that he had thought our vacation had been ideal and he had absolutely no idea why I was raging. He had spent quite a lot of money and had been expecting a tear-filled goodbye full of gratitude for all his effort. What he was witnessing was just bizarre.

"Slap across the face – put you through? What are you talking about? I thought we had a good time."

"Oh, so that's all this is – just good times. I'm done with that. The good times are done. Over." I slammed down my purse for effect and struggled with my seatbelt so I could bolt from the car.

He grabbed my hand to stop me. "Kirsten, you can't leave like this. What the hell is going on?"

"Fine. You want to make me say it? YOU WANT ME TO SAY IT? Why won't you fucking propose?" I screamed. There. That's it. I was done.

"You expected me to propose? Now? But we never talked about that."

"Now – yes. Last month in Paris, yes. The time before that, yes. I've been expecting you to propose during every damn visit since you agreed to stay with me forever. I can't take this anymore. You have to stop toying with me." The tears were welling up.

Seeing the oncoming tears was a good sign that my anger and irrational outbursts were subsiding. He used the window of restored calm to explain that while he meant everything he had said about our future together and intention to marry, we were apparently operating on two very different time lines and he had no idea that I was expecting him to propose now.

"How could I propose when I don't have a ring? Aren't we supposed to go shopping together for that?"

"Of course not!" I was exasperated. "How could you surprise me if we bought it together?"

"But I don't know your ring size. Or what you like. How could I buy something without your help?" It was maddening the way this was turning out, but it certainly could have been worse. At least I was finally making real progress. The downside was that I was forced to let go of the fantasy.

"I'm a size five, I like traditional settings, and you're going to propose to me on New Year's Eve in Paris. Agreed?"

"Agreed."

My fantasy was squashed, but the waiting was finally over.

Brian held up his end of the bargain and proposed on New Year's Eve, just before 2003 turned to 2004, in his apartment in Paris. We were married August 14, 2004 and six months later I was pregnant with our first child Lauren. Baby number two, Alexandra, was soon to follow. Both girls were born in Athens, Greece, our first diplomatic assignment together as a married couple.

Brian emphatically refused to have a third baby, leaving us a happy family of four —me, two little healthy blondie daughters, and a dad that's terrified to have these beauties reach their teens. In fact, a Syrian friend in Athens took one look at our girls and said to Brian in complete seriousness, "you're lucky, you'll be able to marry those two off early."

Until then, Brian and I are muddling through the ups and downs of parenthood, positioning ourselves to provide every possible advantage to our two precious little girls as we try to forge lasting family memories, somehow managing to form a solid, loving, mutually-dependent marriage bond to carry us through the struggles we were unknowingly about to face in Africa.

CHAPTER 5

The Party – The Morning Rush
Rocky Roads and Bouncy Castles

The chanting has started. Loud, lacking rhythm or tune, it thunders from its low-quality speakers, growing louder by the minute. This background noise that has managed to seep into my dream begins to take over until my eyes inevitably open. I turn to grab my watch on my bedside table, but can't read the time because it's too dark. We can't keep that handy, standard clock radio with glow in the dark numbers that we all take for granted next to the bed - too many blackouts, brownouts, electricity cuts. Here, you'd spend all your time re-adjusting the clock, and oversleeping.

'Well, I'm awake now, so I might as well use the bathroom,' I mutter to myself as I stumble out of bed. I bring my watch with me and see by the dim bathroom vanity light that it's 3:30am. So much for the lazy weekend sleep-ins, I think as I groggily turn on the bathroom sink faucet to wash my hands. Nothing. I try again. Great, no water. That means the city supply is down and our back up tank is either dry or not working properly. Brian had checked the backup tank the night before and said it was more than half full with

water, so the problem must be mechanical. The last time this happened, it took two weeks to repair.

Lauren wanders her way into the bathroom to see what's going on. Was I grumbling that loudly?

"Mommy, the singer woke me up. Can I play?"

"No honey. It's really early. Try to go back to sleep."

"Can I sleep with you?" I'm about to say yes when I see Alexandra making her way towards us. We don't have enough room in our tiny embassy-provided bed to accommodate four, so I have to change my answer.

"No, Lauren. You know the rules. No kids in our bed until the sun comes up."

"But I can't sleep. The noise is too loud again."

"Mommy?" Alexandra is with Lauren and me in the bathroom now; three people in the mold-smelling bathroom at 3:30am, trying to block out the sounds of the Ethiopian Orthodox Church loudspeakers. "Can I have some cake?"

"No Alexandra, no party cake until after lunch."

"But mommy, why is there no ice cream? Emma says you're supposed to have ice cream with cake at parties and we never have ice cream."

Emma is their new friend who just arrived in Ethiopia from America.

"Yes, Emma's right. But ice cream is too expensive for us. You need a freezer to keep ice cream cold and the electricity is always stopping here." I could go on to say that if stores want to keep their ice cream from melting, they have to buy expensive generators and fuel them with expensive imported diesel fuel to guarantee electricity coverage during the many times the city's power is cut, which means that ice cream is way out of our price league. But it's 3:30 in the morning and I don't have the energy to lapse into a rant with my four year old.

"I wish I had ice cream. Emma says there's not just chocolate, strawberry, and vanilla, but so many other kinds. Like bubble gum. Mommy, can I have bubble gum ice cream one day?" Alexandra's eyes are starting to widen with anticipation.

"Oh, yeah, and mommy," Lauren chimes in, "Emma says her favorite is Rocky Road. Rocky Road! Isn't that funny. A funny, funny joke. You don't eat a rocky road, that's what you drive on, right mommy? Why would you put the rocky road into ice cream? Emma is so silly."

"Well, Rocky Road is a super silly name, but Emma's right, it's also a yummy ice cream flavor. I kind of forget, but I think it is vanilla with lots of chocolate, caramel, and maybe nuts and marshmallows."

"No way!" they both yell out in unison, unable to believe their ears – could such an amazing thing actually exist? "We want Rocky Road, not the ones outside, the ice cream! We want Rocky Road, not the ones outside, the ice cream!" They start chanting, and I can't help but join in.

When they eventually bore of their new song, after about four verses, Lauren becomes very serious and asks, "Really mommy, can we have it?"

"Yes, of course. We'll buy some when we move back to America next weekend. America is the land of ice cream. Can you believe it - there are hundreds of flavors to choose from….." I think of Ben and Jerry's coffee health bar crunch and start to salivate.

"Really? Really, really? You have enough money to buy us ice cream?" both Lauren and Alexandra are squealing and jumping up and down now. Alexandra even starts spinning in a little circle with her arms flared out at the sides. This is some serious excitement.

"Hey, keep it down in there. You're louder than the church," Brian protests from the bedroom.

"Bad move Brian, I can't protect you now."

"Daddy!" the kids leave me to sprint for dad. By now, it's approaching 3:45 and the kids are jumping on Brian's stomach, yelling "ice cream, ice cream, ice cream!"

A typical weekend morning. For some reason, the girls have Brian's job as a diplomat confused with him being a professional wrestler, and it is their duty to condition him for battle every weekend morning.

"Ok, ok kids, that's enough. Back to bed, let daddy rest. Come back when the sun's up. Rules."

"Oh, maaan. We never get to do annnnythhiiing," Lauren whines as the two get down off the bed and start walking back to their room.

Alexandra looks back over her shoulder, "can we go to the pool today?"

"Nope, it's a party today."

"How about the water fountain?" Next to the pool, their favorite weekend activity is to go to the newly built U.S. Embassy and drink out of the water fountains. A big novelty.

"Nope again. Today is the party we're having here at our house all day for everyone. Fasika, Tigist, Shibru, Tesfaye, Mesfin, and Getahun. So we can say goodbye."

"Oh maaaan."

"Yeah, we never get to do anything."

And then they're gone. Followed by blissful silence. It's 4:00am and the Ethiopian Orthodox Church speakers appear to be finished, for now. But five o'clock belongs to Islam – it marks the Muslim's morning call to prayer. And our house has the good fortune of being located right in the middle of the two. It's like being seated at a table between dueling pianos (competing for your soul at the crack of dawn) when all you want is a quiet meal (or one lazy, restful weekend morning).

Somehow we all manage to go back to sleep and I at least don't notice the mosque's call to worship. The kids wake up with the sun at around six am and make their way downstairs to their playroom, to the TV room to watch cartoons, to the office to play video games, to the living room with the DVD player, and outside to use our swing set and kids club house. It all usually keeps them occupied until I get out of bed around 8:00. But today I'm up before 7:00am frantically making ice cubes using bottled water so that guests can put ice with potable water in their drinks.

"What are you doing?" Brian asks with a puzzled expression as he walks into the kitchen and sees me pouring bottled water into our ice cube trays.

"I'm making eatable ice. I completely forgot and we only have five hours to make enough for all the guests."

"Kirsten, Ethiopians don't like cold drinks. They think it gives them sore throats, remember?"

"Oh. I forgot." We sent Fasika to an embassy-recommended hospital once to get medicine for strep throat. It wasn't easy – her mistrust for hospitals, doctors, and medicine is ingrained. She resisted for a couple of days, insisting her pain was from drinking cold water and that it the problem would soon go away. In the end, she went with Brian to the hospital, was tested, and was given medicine to cure her advanced case of strep.

Lauren and Alexandra hear us talking and come into the kitchen. "Ok, so we're going to the pool today, right?" little miss Lauren thinks she might pull a fast one over on us. Alexandra just stands next to Lauren with her hands on her hips and says "yeah."

"Nope, but how about a bath?" I offer up to avoid confrontation.

"Yippee, a bath," my two water babies blurt out together, stripping off their clothes as they make their way for the stairs.

"Wait, wait, let me check your ringworm first," I say as I walk toward Lauren - a perfect opportunity to examine her now that her pajama top is off. I turn her arm over and see the faint red outline of a small circle. "Almost gone. Did daddy put the cream on last night?"

"Yee-eess mom. Can I go now?"

"Ok, but don't put the water in your mouth. Lauren, Alexandra, promise. No bath tub water in your mouths. I don't want any booboo tummies today."

Lauren's third bout of ringworm and talk of booboo tummies from drinking Addis Ababa's untreated bath water reminds me of when we first arrived in Ethiopia and took the girls to the U.S. Embassy Halloween party dressed in their adorable Pottery Barn pumpkin costumes. Alexandra's body was lightly spotted with little red dots, but I wrote them off as an attack of mosquitoes. She had been susceptible to bug bites and mosquitoes while living in Greece, so this was nothing new. But what we didn't think about was that Alexandra was too young to have been fully vaccinated against chicken pox before coming to Addis Ababa. She had had just one of a series of shots, leaving her vulnerable to the disease that apparently is prevalent throughout Ethiopia.

After a full day of mingling with other kids and having her chubby cheeks pinched by gushing adults, it turns out that we were the culprits of an embassy-wide chicken pox outbreak. Oops. My consolation is that at least she had been fully vaccinated against yellow fever, typhoid, and polio before hitting the ground in Ethiopia at age two.

"Mom! Moooooom!" The kids are screaming from their bathroom upstairs. Oh yeah, no water. Oops again.

"Who wants cake?" I yell back. Ok, so I'm not the best mom.

I turn to Brian. *"Can you call to have the water pump fixed again?"*

"Really?"

"Really."

The morning rolls by and soon it's nine o'clock. The kids are dressed, teeth brushed, hair brushed, and they've had some cereal with their favorite imported powdered milk. How I long to give them fresh milk one day, from cows that aren't infected with tuberculosis.

Still overly anxious about the party food, I send Brian out to the restaurant to check on the order even though the agreed upon pick up isn't until eleven am. Brian starts to respond with an incredulous look, but then shrugs his shoulders. *"Sure, why not?"* And out the door he goes, just a little too eager to have an excuse to get out of the house.

With Brian now gone to take care of the food, I begin to fixate on the bouncy castle I rented for all the kids, particularly my housekeeper Tigist's little girl Blen. The one I had ordered for today's party is ridiculously expensive and huge - with a slide and climbing wall, the works. The castle and its operators are supposed to be at the house by ten am. It's still early, but I start to think of the many "no problem" scenarios and I really don't want to disappoint the kids today, particularly Blen. Apparently, she had been talking about this "bouncy castle party" for weeks — to her friends, classmates, family,

*strangers, dogs, cats, donkeys, goats, sheep, long-horned oxen —
basically anything in her vicinity that has ears.*

*I dig into my purse for the bouncy castle company's scribbled cell
phone number. No harm in calling just to reconfirm that they're on
the way. I pull out my mobile and dial the number. It rings, someone
answers, and then the 'no network' beeps, cutting us off before I even
say hello.*

*Ok, I still have options. There's the scribbled website address
written below the cell phone number. I turn on my computer. I press
connect when prompted, and I wait. And I wait. The connection is
wavering between zero kpbs and 40 kbps. It's painful.*

*I walk outside to check on the kids as they eat their small slices
of "breakfast" bribery cake while playing on the swing. Fasika is
with them, having arrived just after Brian left, and they're all giggling
about touching the clouds with their feet.*

*All is good, so I go back to the office to check the internet.
It's connected. I type in the address and wait some more. The speed
has picked up slightly, and the bouncy castle site emerges on screen. It
shows pictures of their castles, lots of happy kids, gives prices, a cell
phone contact number, and that's it. For some reason I had been
hoping to find an address so that I could call Brian and ask him to
swing by their shop. Oh well, I'll try again to call the place instead. I
dial the number and connect right away. Someone answers and I say
hello. We go back and forth for a minute, but the language barrier is*

*too challenging, so I make my way back outside and hand the phone
to Fasika.*

*Fasika takes the mobile and begins berating the bouncy castle
guy for being late (even though it's still only 9:25am). She pulls out
her forceful tone, attacking the bouncy castle man as if she's taking
out her frustrations with all men on this one poor guy. But it works.
Within 20 minutes, he's in my yard and setting up the huge castle.
Fasika stands watch over him with eagle eyes to make sure he doesn't
shirk his duties, work too slowly, or in any other way step out of line.*

*Just as he's finalizing the last touches, putting in pegs on the
corners so the castle doesn't topple, there's a knock at the door. I
walk over to open the gate as the bouncy castle guy flips the on switch,
the massive toy coming to life with giant bursts of air. Wondering who
this early bird guest might be, I swing open the gate door to find
Tigist, my housekeeper, and her excited little girl Blen.*

Tigist says hello and explains that she came early to help.

*"No way. There will be no work for the two of you today. No
arguments." But perhaps helping wasn't the only reason for Tigist's –
and by that I mean her daughter Blen's – early arrival.*

*"Madame. Madame." I turn from greeting Tigist to look down
at the beaming little face of a stunning seven-year old girl as she tugs
on my arm for attention. To mark today's occasion, Blen is decked
out in her best white dress that is teeming with ruffles and ribbons,*

seemingly in intense competition for space on the oversized dress draping this frail girl's stunted frame.

"Well hello there beautiful," I beam back at her as I bend down to give the adorable little girl a big hug.

"Me play?! Me play?!" she squeals, pointing to the huge blow-up bouncy castle that is now up and blowing at full capacity, with my two girls already jumping like maniacs inside.

"Of course. Today, it is all for you!" But she's off before I finish my sentence, bows and ribbons trailing in her wake. Watching her go, it is hard to imagine that just over two years ago this little girl had been starving and on the verge of death deep in Ethiopia's countryside.

CHAPTER 6

Tigist – Adoption, Ethiopian Style

"The beauty of the world has two edges, one of laughter, one of anguish, cutting the heart asunder." - *Virginia Wolf*

The fateful day began two years ago when Tigist boarded a bus that was leaving Ethiopia's capital city for a remote area home to a revered Orthodox church. The journey is long and arduous, with people crammed into the dilapidated bus that lacks air circulation as it bumps along the country's rough, dirt roads.

Reaching its destination after hours of being jostled about on the bus' wooden bench seats, the bus off-loads its passengers in front of the imposing church. As the pilgrims resolutely file off the bus, straightening their stiff backs and stretching legs to slowly regain circulation, they immediately bend over in religious zeal upon sight of the massive and elaborate structure rising like a phoenix out of the otherwise bleak and desolate landscape.

Walking closer to the divine building, the Addis Ababa passengers pass throngs of beggars lining the road, shivering in Ethiopia's cold mountain dampness as they wait in anticipation for alms from the privileged pilgrims that can afford the bus journey from their county's mystical, faraway capital. To them, according to Tigist, Ethiopia's capital of Addis Ababa is an almost mythical place that provincial villagers imagine to be "paved with gold."

As Tigist walks along the path leading to the church, in step behind the other pilgrims, one particular beggar woman with an infant and toddler in tow catches her eye. Tigist later told me that she couldn't explain what exactly had caused her to notice this one woman above the many others, but the image of her and her two hollow-cheeked children - scantily dressed in dirty scraps of cloth and shivering in their listless mother's arms - stayed with her as she entered the church to pray.

Later that afternoon, as Tigist was descending the church's crumbling steps, she was surprised to see that the beggar woman and her two children were among the few beggars still lingering along the roadside. Given this second chance for an encounter, Tigist determined it to be a sign from God and she approached the woman.

Speaking in Amharic, Tigist hands the mother a few Birr, saying, "Please, take this small amount for your children." The woman takes the money with no acknowledgement, wearing a vacant expression that to Tigist resembled living death. The baby begins to cry while the toddler rallies all her strength to reach out and stroke Tigist's shiny black purse.

"You like it? Look, you can see your reflection." Tigist raises the purse to the girl's face, rewarded by a slight smile that doesn't quite manage to reach the hungry child's eyes. "What's your name?"

The baby is still crying, the mother taking little interest. The girl creeps closer to her mom, unsure about Tigist's attention.

"Don't be scared," Tigist says, flashing her most reassuring smile before turning her focus to the mother. "What's her name?" No answer. Tigist reaches back into her shiny purse for a few more Birr. "What's your name?"

she asks the mother, holding up the equivalent of about fifty cents.

"Mahlet," is the weak, disinterested, and barely audible reply.

"Mahlet, I'm Tigist. Can you tell me about you? I want to help." Tigist doesn't know where she's going with this, but she can't stop. She feels eerily drawn to this woman and her two girls and is driven to learn more.

After a little more coaxing, Mahlet tells Tigist that she is from a tiny, distant village of a few clustered huts. She has never been to school nor has any member of her family as far back as she can recall. She used to live in a one room, circular hovel of mud walls with a thatched roof - a primitive Ethiopian dwelling called a tukul - with her husband's extended family. They had no electricity and no running water. No one in the village did. Often, there was no food.

One day, after an argument with her husband, the husband left this woman and the two children, saying he was headed for Ethiopia's capital city in search of gold and would not return. Because the husband's family didn't feel the need to allow this discarded woman and her two abandoned children to stay in the hut in the husband's absence, taking up precious space and consuming scarce food, they summarily expelled the scorned family.

Homeless and hungry, with no access to income and two children to feed, the woman's only option was to beg.

The woman's life story complete, Tigist took out her cell phone and called her parents, with whom she lives in Addis Ababa, to ask if it will be ok to bring home a child. After several attempts, she finally connected and her parents agreed. Tigist then asked the woman if Tigist could take the toddler girl, explaining that this would relieve Mahlet of part of her burden.

Because Tigist assured Mahlet that she would feed the child and send her to school, the mother eventually agreed, but only on the condition that Tigist help her and her infant also get to this mythical Addis Ababa.

Tigist boarded the bus that was waiting to take its pilgrim passengers back to the capital. Standing at the front, she declared, "This woman wants to go with us to Addis Ababa. I will pay the bus fare. Who else can help? She needs a job and can work as a housekeeper. She does not need a salary, only food and shelter for her and her baby. Who will help save this woman and her children from starving?"

Tigist's plea was met by silence, followed by fervent murmurings. After what seemed like an eternity to Tigist as she clutched Mahlet's little girl closely to her side, someone finally shouted out, "Yes, I will take them. But she must work hard. Food is not cheap."

Relieved, Tigist helped Mahlet and the two children get settled on the floor in the aisle at the back of the bus. They huddled together on the bus' floor, the mother's face frozen in a firm expression of false pride, although at a closer look, Tigist saw that her wide eyes gave away her curiosity and fear.

As the bus started to begin its journey back to Addis, an anxious Mahlet drew her children nearer. Over time, they adjusted to the sensation of movement, to the noises, to the passing scenery. As beggars, the family had seen the occasional bus or car, but they had never conceived of ever being inside of one of the monster-like machines.

After many hours, they finally arrived in Addis Ababa. Tigist gave Mahlet her cell phone number and took the girl. Transaction final. Adoption complete.

Considered a selfless act of charity, this type of adoption is not uncommon in Ethiopia. It rescues children from a life of suffering and perhaps starvation. It's a manifestation of the Ethiopian peoples' generous spirit, but it's also a stark example of the ruthlessness of poverty, creating scenarios where mothers find themselves giving their children to strangers in a base act of survival.

ഇഇരുരു

A few months pass and Tigist receives a call from Mahlet.

"I want my girl. You cannot have her."

Startled by this unexpected demand, Tigist is silent as Mahlet continues. "I am sick. I need my girl. She helps me. You cannot take her from me. Bring her back."

Tigist refuses. At this point, Tigist has introduced the child into a stable household that lives in a permanent structure and eats fairly nutritious, regular meals; has intermittent access to electricity, a television, and radio; and Tigist is even able to provide the girl access to some preschool education. Not but five months earlier, this same child had been in charge of watching goats all day, eating a meal once daily, and living in a cramped, one room hut. By the time Tigist discovered her, she was homeless and starving. Tigist tells Mahlet not to call again and hangs up the phone.

A few more weeks go by and Tigist receives another desperate call from the mother. This time, Mahlet says that she quit the house where she had been living and is now staying at the Mother Theresa Foundation. She is very sick and longs to see her daughter again before she dies.

Responding to the mothers' desperation, Tigist relents and brings the daughter to the Foundation. Walking into the charity's compound with the child, Tigist greets an attendant. "We're here to visit Mahlet. She is sick and wants to see this girl. Can you please tell us where we can find Mahlet?"

"Mahlet? Let me check. One moment." The attendant walks out into the nearby ward. Returning fifteen minutes later, she informs Tigist in a matter-of-fact tone, "Mahlet is in the HIV/AIDs ward in the back. Bed number 52."

Tigist's heart sinks as a wave of panic surges through her body. When she eventually finds Mahlet in bed number 52 after navigating the labyrinth of hospital beds, she is faced with a terribly thin, weak, and feeble shell of a person, folds of lipid skin hanging off her hollow cheeks, unable to care for her infant who had been taken from her to be nursed in a different section of the compound.

"Mahlet, when did you get AIDS?" Tigist pleads. The mother shrugs. "Do you know who, how? Anything?" Tigist's frantic battery of questions is met with shrugs. Getting nowhere, Tigist has the daughter immediately tested and with much relief learns that both the daughter and infant are negative.

Mahlet made a slow recovery under the care of the Mother Theresa Foundation. Having herself now been 'adopted' by an anonymous Mother Theresa Foundation donor, she now has access to life sustaining, anti-retroviral medication, is able to pay rent in a one-room Addis Ababa slum dwelling, and can afford a daily meal for herself and her growing baby.

With renewed strength and settled in the city under the assistance of a charity, Tigist confides to me that Mahlet continues to try to reclaim her daughter. The daughter, however, is thriving under Tigist's care. She's a healthy, well-adjusted, good student who says she does not want to return to her mother. Her mother has little recourse to pursue custody, being poor, illiterate, and marginalized. At the same time, Tigist has no legal right to keep the child and fears that she could be snatched away at any time.

It's a difficult story to digest and you feel for both sides, as right and wrong becomes skewed under the heavy weight of basic survival, where solutions defy simple logic, and where everyday life is closely entwined with a primitive closeness to life and death.

And Brian was about to experience this first hand.

CHAPTER 7

The Party – Ten O'Clock
Ring Road Perils

It's ten o'clock and my cell phone rings. Brian.

"No. Don't tell me, don't tell me." Fasika and Tigist and Tigist's daughter Blen are already here and other hungry guests will be coming in a few hours. I need that food.

"Calm down," Brian cuts me off before I spiral into panic. "It's all here, and early I might add. They're just finishing last minute things and packing up. I'll be leaving soon, back by ten thirty at the latest."

Forty-five minutes go by. Brian calls again.

"Tell me you're at the goat corner."

Silence. Something is wrong. Brian's voice waivers. "I hit a child."

෬෬ᏏᏏ

The Ring Road

Given the deplorable road and chaotic driving conditions in Addis, the city is plagued by a car accident curse that dictates you cannot survive a diplomatic assignment in Ethiopia without being involved in some kind of a car accident. One hopes the inevitable incident will be minor. Sometimes it involves a pedestrian. Occasionally, it results in death. With virtually no medical care, even minor car accident-induced injuries can be fatal.

In an effort to alleviate city congestion and improve the abhorrent driving conditions, the city planned and built a ring road to divert some of the urban traffic. In the end, after years of construction, the much anticipated beltway is finally complete. Well, that's not entirely accurate. Better to say that construction has permanently stopped and the city has a partially functioning ring road, with one section of what should have been the ring never to be completed. Somehow, during the planning phases, it is said that apparently all had overlooked the minor detail that this one remaining section of the road would cut directly through the British Embassy compound. Realizing the mistake too late, plans were changed to build an overpass above the embassy. That also didn't go over well with the Brits, and the city is now left with its little-used ring road.

People generally opt to overlook this virtually useless highway except when they find themselves in a desperate hurry. While this ring road at times can provide a quick alternative to navigating dense, chaotic city traffic, it is so little used by cars that animals and people have migrated in to fill the space. From sleeping cows, to soccer games, to abandoned cars and trucks left in the middle of the highway, you never know what you'll encounter on the ring road. But unlike the crazed city conditions that limit your speed, it is possible to reach speeds of up to 60 mph on the ring, and the combination can be deadly.

In spite of the ring road dangers, Brian opts to take the ring road today so that he can get home earlier. As he approached a bend in the highway, a soccer ball rolled out in front of the car. This ball was immediately followed by a little boy. It all happened too quickly. Brian swerved, but it turned out that he had swerved his car in the same direction that the boy lunged in his panic. The boy was hit. He looked no older than three.

As is customary, Brian put the boy in his car to take him to the nearest hospital. There are no ambulances to call and there were no adults in sight.

While helping the little boy inside his SUV, Brian was relieved to see that the boy seemed to be ok, probably just a tap and a scare. To Brian's credit and good judgment, he had been driving slowly and it luckily had not been a direct hit.

Just as Brian was strapping in the seatbelts to leave the scene for the hospital, the boy's mother showed up, having been alerted by other children who had witnessed the accident. The mother appeared surprisingly calm for someone whose child has just been hit by a car.

She indicated to Brian that she wanted to take the boy home with her.

Brian called the embassy operator on his cell phone for translation assistance, and luckily was able to connect on his second try. He informed the operator of the situation and asked that the operator explain to the mother in Amharic that he was going to take the boy to the nearest hospital and that although the boy seemed to be ok, it was important to move quickly.

"No hospital," the mother replied emphatically to Brian.

The mother was slight in stature, she had high cheekbones and a weathered face. It was impossible to gauge her age. She was illiterate, uneducated, and gravely suspicious.

The operator assured her that Brian would pay the bill, but the woman continued to resist.

The operator told Brian that the woman preferred to have the boy go to a neighborhood "doctor," someone she trusted, who has "the necessary potions to remove evil spirits."

Owing to the operator's patience and persistent engagement, Brian's continued insistence eventually paid off and the mother finally relented. The next step was to coax her into the car, an obvious first for the woman and another source of deeply suspicious concern. Once accomplished, with the mother and the boy finally in the car, Brian drove to a hospital.

The hospital building was a rundown structure, barely lit, with smudged walls and emitting a putrid smell. There was an Addis University trained doctor on hand; a tired looking man with few of the resources you would expect to see in a doctor's office. But he represented the closest thing to modern medical care available and was clearly a better option than the neighborhood keeper of spells.

The doctor conducted a cursory exam and said the boy, who was six years old - not three as Brian had thought, was fine. Relieved, Brian drove the boy and his mom back to their neighborhood and dropped them off near the scene of the accident. As Brian watched them get out of the car to walk back to their tin-roofed shack, he couldn't help but wonder why a little boy of six years, who was stunted to look much younger than his actual age, had been left alone to play soccer on a highway.

He put the car in drive and pulled out his cell phone to call me to let me know what had happened.

෩෩ CฌCฌ

Not knowing what was taking so long and again unable to reach Brian on the faulty cell phone network, I had to do something. By now, it was almost 11 o'clock, the time I had asked people to arrive, and I had nothing to offer guests to eat.

Fasika offers to see if she can find anything to buy in the neighborhood tin shops that line the dirt road outside of my house. Reluctant to rely on Fasika yet again, especially today, I tell her that

I'll go. Fasika glares back at me like a scolding mother and points out that I won't know what to buy, where to buy it, how to buy it or how much to pay. Foreigners are not meant to do these things, she says to me with a mere look, and I relent.

I hang my head in shame. I've got nothing. Yes, after nearly three years living here, I can't even buy food on my own. In fact, I have taken only one disastrous "leisure" walk outside of my fence in all this time. I went around the block with my kids one afternoon soon after arriving in Ethiopia and never ventured out for a "pleasure walk" again. Instead, just like every other expat foreigner I know, I buy my food at the few stores that cater to foreigners with shockingly high price tags, I walk around the track at the International School, I lounge at the Sheraton pool on weekends or at the home of friends, and I shuttle myself to and from everywhere I need to be by car.

Dejected at my failure to adapt beyond my work outreach activities, I give Fasika money and thank her profusely. With her help, we should have some food before the rest of the guests arrive. Fasika again saves the day.

But just two minutes after Fasika left my home's compound, Brian calls again. He just saw Fasika walking past the corner goat market toward the banana stand manned by the old blind guy. He picked her up before she bought anything, and he tells me they are one minute from the house with a car full of food. Brian's uneven voice reveals that he's pretty shaken.

In Ethiopia, you just never know what can happen around each corner, around each bend in the road. Worlds can be turned upside down and inside out in an instant. It's enough to make you lose your smile. I remember the day when my smile disappeared.

CHAPTER 8

Addis Ababa – A Beautiful Day in the Neighborhood

"The world is a great book….they who never stir from home read only a page." - St. Augustine

Ethiopia is a country known for its gentle and beautiful people, with tourism guidebook slogans proclaiming the country to be "the land of a thousand smiles" that enjoys "thirteen months of sunshine." It is a fascinating place, shrouded in mystery – dating all the way back to the Old Testament. It is home to towering obelisks, the revered land of the Queen of Sheba, rumored to house the Ark of the Covenant, and a region that practiced Christianity long before much of Europe. "From the source of the Blue Nile to the enigmatic relics of Axum, Gondor, and Lalibela to the scorching infernal of the Danakali depression, the wonders of the Simien and Bale Mountains, and the game-filled wilderness of the remote southern grassland," Ethiopia's tourism guides unabashedly and unequivocally proclaim Ethiopia to be "an odyssey of discovery."

Reading these descriptions before coming to Africa, I was gripped by excitement over what adventures and experiences lay ahead for me and my family in this exotic land. Conveying my excitement to friends and family in the U.S., however – those like my homebody sister Jenny who is unfamiliar with Ethiopia beyond the televised faces of starving children from the mid-1980s famine – proved to be my first challenge.

"No, really, we're very excited. You should read some of these travel magazines. Check out this picture," I say, almost begging Jenny for her acceptance and support as I point to the glossy photo of a breathtaking Blue Nile waterfall. "And don't forget, Ethiopia is a relatively crime-free place to raise a family – safer than Washington, DC."

"Ok, so what do you do when one of your girls comes down with malaria? Really, you want to expose your kids to all those diseases?"

"Jenny, Addis Ababa, the capital where we'll live, rests at about 8,000 feet," I retort in my most exasperated and condescending tone. "At that elevation, Brian and I may drop dead of heart attacks, but there's no chance of malaria."

Inevitably, though, just as I would be about to win over my audiences and alleviate their concerns, my funny-man husband would interject with his version of a geography 101 lesson of the Horn of Africa: "Ethiopia is just west of Somalia (think Black Hawk Down), just east of Sudan (Darfur), a little south-west of Yemen (Osama bin-Ladin's ancestral home and site of the USS Cole bombing), and a little north-east of Rwanda (think 1990's genocide). Oh, and two U.S. embassies a little south-east of Ethiopia were blown up in a 1990's Al-Qaeda terrorist attack (Kenya and Tanzania)."

His overview was always met with stunned, horrified expressions. But sophomoric antics aside, perhaps Brian was on to something. As I proceeded to read books and articles on Ethiopia to become better acquainted with my future home - studying the country's history, updating myself on current events and the state of political affairs, and talking to people - I learned that the Horn of Africa is a tough neighborhood. I learned that life is never easy for the poor, and the poor in tough neighborhoods particularly suffer. But what I had yet to discover was that none of this reading or arm chair analysis could adequately prepare me for what it really feels like to be confronted head on by the wretched squalor that accompanies abject poverty in a place like Ethiopia.

Ethiopia is a place where 12 million people out of an estimated population of 77 million are at risk of starvation on a regular basis. Chronic malnutrition is pervasive. According to U.S. government figures, Ethiopia has one of the world's lowest rates of access to safe water supply, sanitation, and hygiene despite an abundant supply of ground and surface water resources. In 2007, mortality rates for children under the age of five, according to UNICEF, were approximately 119 out of every 1,000 live births. UNICEF also reports that with nearly 400,000 children under five still dying each year from preventable causes such as diarrhea, Ethiopia continues to have one of the highest child mortality rates in the world.

It's not that Ethiopia's tourism guidebooks are wrong, or that my excitement over moving to this country was misplaced or misguided. From its ancient history, captivating landscapes, and alluring and diverse cultures, the country truly is an odyssey of discovery. If only I could get past the wretchedness of poverty.

ഇഇൿൿ

During one afternoon a few weeks into my arrival in Ethiopia, at a time when I was feeling particularly claustrophobic - trapped yet another day inside my home's walled compound - I blurted out to Fasika while we were both in my kitchen preparing the kids' lunch, "Fasika, why did you come back to Ethiopia from Dubai?"

"I love my home. I never leave Ethiopia now."

"What do you love the most? I've been here one month and I don't know anything about this place. Only inside this fence. Inside the Embassy walls. Inside my car."

With that entry, Fasika beamed with excitement at the opportunity to extol the virtues of her homeland. She happily filled my ears with stories of all that Ethiopia has to offer for those willing to take the leap and venture beyond the foreigners' limited, walled-off universe. Fasika described elaborate coffee ceremonies that serve up the best quality coffee in the world, traditional dresses and stunning scarves made of renowned Ethiopian cotton sold in corner shops, intricate silver or wood carved Orthodox crosses that hail from all corners of Ethiopia, imposing churches filled with historic relics, and friendly people eager to talk to foreigners.

Listening to her speak with such pride about her country and its heritage, a nagging obligation to disregard my embassy's security warnings and engage my surrounding environment more directly gained momentum, encouraging me to step outside of the confines of my locked car and to go beyond the security of my fence - to fully become an active participant in my new world. But to really get to know my host home, to move beyond weathered clichés based upon casual observances, I had to break free of the barriers, both real and perceived, that separate me from my new surroundings. I had to take a walk.

It is in this mindset that I finally decide to take my first tentative steps out into the 'real world' on my own. I was ready to experience Ethiopia, or, well, at least get to know my neighborhood a little. And so, while humming the Mr. Rogers theme song on the morning of my "coming out" to my neighbors, I decide to take a leisurely stroll with my kids, toddlers Lauren and Alexandra, around my block.

Soon after heading off on this grand independent adventure with my Graco double stroller that had served me so well on the broken sidewalks of Athens, Greece, I discover that its plastic wheels are no match for Africa's dirt, rocks, potholes, and ditches. But determined to persevere, I keep pushing and soon get used to, maybe even enjoy, the physical struggle. Ethiopia is a hardship assignment, and here I am out and about, pulling my weight with a smile. I keep humming.

Conquering this first obstacle, ridiculous smile still plastered across my face, I take the opportunity to more closely observe my surroundings – which leads to a disturbing discovery. It is the disconcerting way the people I pass look at me. I don't question my safety, but the expressions on the faces of the people I pass are almost frightening. The looks are directed straight to my core with a piercing intensity, as if they are questioning the very fabric of my being with a sort of "how dare you" confrontational challenge.

I try to ignore the looks, deciding that I am probably misreading the expressions based on some subliminal, self-conscious anxiety. But I am markedly less hopeful and I soon stop humming.

I walk past other homes larger than mine, also hidden behind massive security fences that mock the pretty white picket fences of my suburban youth. But in this "mixed" neighborhood that houses people from all walks of life, there are also many make-shift dwellings of mud walls and corrugated tin roofs riddled with gaping holes. Passing by one such dwelling, two un-bathed children with ripped, ill-fitting dresses and runny noses dart out from their lean-to structure and into the dirt road as I pass, pointing at me and giggling with childish innocence before running off again.

I continue strolling and see a half-naked man, covered in only a grimy, brown blanket full of holes draped across his pencil-thin frame, sleeping on the side of the dirt road; I see children tending to a group of goats during what should be their school time, chewing khat to pass the time (a leafy stimulant narcotic popular in eastern Africa); there are men sitting on boxes and drinking beer inside a dark, dirt floor shack that is just big enough to barely contain a damaged pool table; and I pass a vegetable stand with rotting lettuce sitting in the dirt and covered with flies, looked after by an old and withered blind man.

Suddenly, out of nowhere, there's a loud thud. I jump. I turn from gazing at the image of the blind man to look in the direction of the thump. Lauren is trying to wrangle herself out of the stroller to pick up a large, bloody bone dripping with bits of flesh that apparently had just dropped from the sky to land in front of us, just off to the right side of the road. I look up to the sky to see a massive vulture swooping over our heads, the talons wrapped around a rancid feast of flesh-covered bones.

In my few weeks living in my new neighborhood, I had become accustomed to the sight of these giant, gangly, repulsive creatures given the proximity of our home to the city of Addis Ababa's slaughter house. The birds gather there in massive numbers, covering the bone-studded hillside with their grotesque bodies as they feast on discarded, rotting animal flesh in a daily demonstration of frenzied gluttony.

But on this particular day, at this particular time – as I was taking my first neighborhood walk around the block with my kids – this particular carrion-eating bird flying over our heads had decided to take his rancid slaughter house feast to go. Having apparently been overly greedy, though, he couldn't handle the full extent of his bounty. It was our lucky day (or so Lauren and Alexandra believed) that the bird dropped one of the bloody bones nearly at our feet as it flew overhead. It was all I could do to keep my squealing toddlers belted in their stroller, their little fingers off what they somehow saw as a cool treasure sent tumbling from the sky, delivered directly to them for their personal enjoyment. Oddly, no one else walking along the dirt road seemed to take any notice. To them, my girls and I were a much greater anomaly.

At this point, Lauren had almost unstrapped herself. Tenacious to her core, there is no stopping Lauren when she wants something, so I desperately needed a distraction. I had the perfect idea. The goats! Just up ahead on the corner, in the direction of home, was our corner sheep and goat market.

"Hey guys, wanna say hello to the goats?" I said with all the enthusiasm I could muster as I pointed to the busy corner.

Alexandra answered with a huge smile and loud "bah" noises. Lauren was more dubious, looking from the fetid bone to the goats and back again.

"Oh, come on Lauren. That bone stinks. It's filthy and will make you sick. Those goats are so cute and really want to say hello to you. Just listen to them." With that, Alexandra starts clapping and Lauren gives in and adds to the "bah" cacophony.

We approach the corner slowly as I plan my strategy for communicating to the teen shepherds that my girls would like to pet their goats. The group of twenty or so goats and sheep begin to nervously bleat as we get closer, their large black eyes staring at us as they stomp in place, their hoofed feet kicking up clouds of brown dust. My cough catches the attention of one of the red-eyed teens who looks over my way with a bored expression.

I pull the stroller alongside the circle of goats so Lauren and Alexandra can reach out and touch the sheep's and goat's matted, flea-infested coats. The teen grabs the closest goat by his front two legs and lurches it at us. I try to smile, saying no, it's ok, the girls are fine petting the ones they can reach. The teen thrusts the goat closer to me, still holding the front two legs in a vice grip, and pulls it up into the air. The goat lets out a shriek of pain and my girls begin to cry.

"Ok, ok." I say to the guy. And by that, I mean, 'put the poor goat down and we'll pet him.'

The teen puts the goat down, but instead of letting us pet it, he holds the goat's head in an odd position and reaches into his pocket. That's when I notice a large pile of mounting bloody carcasses sitting just next to the huddle of sheep and goats, in the shade cast by a corner shack selling CDs and decorated with a giant poster of Shakira. I see the glint of steel coming out of the shepherd's pocket and realize that he's about to slit the goat's throat. Right there, in front of me, in front of the girls.

"No! No!" I yell and rip the stroller around so the girls won't see the slaughter that's about to unfold. The teen takes this as a sign that I'm going back on the sale. He stops what he's about to do and instead comes after me, indicating with hand gestures and some broken English that I can choose another goat, we can change the price. I wonder if he'll follow me all the way back to my house and I step up my pace, never looking back despite my girls disappointed cries that they didn't get to say goodbye to their "Mr. Goatie Friends."

With all the commotion, the goats and sheep start to wander, and the teen shepherd is forced to go back to his corner, whipping the animals back to their corner market spot.

Having just barely averted my children witnessing a primordial scene of goat throat slitting on this dirt road, out of nowhere I am forced to lunge into the roadside's gutter, stroller and all, to avoid being hit by a large SUV with UN letters etched prominently on its side as it comes barreling down the dirt road, kicking up a massive cloud of choking brown dust in its wake. As the dust from the only car I encounter on my entire walk resettles, I struggle to get the double stroller out of the gutter and back onto the road and I notice that Lauren has again perked up from her perch at the front end of the stroller, pointing at something straight ahead. What now, I lament to myself as my enthusiasm for this walk is markedly waning.

"Mommy, why is that man peeing in the road?" Lauren asks as we pass, well, a man peeing in the road. "Is he pretending to be a doggie too?" she asks with mounting excitement.

At this time, my "spirited" little Lauren was at the end stages of potty training and took a perverse pleasure in peeing in our yard. Being in the process of transitioning out of diapers, I definitely preferred her accidents to occur outside in the yard versus inside the house. But in my

Lauren's case, these were no accidents, just another one of Lauren's exasperating phases – she wants to be a doggie and doggies go pee pee outside.

"No sweetie. I think he needs to use the potty very badly, but there are no toilets for him nearby."

"Oh. Can I go pee pee there too, please?" She asks, bounding with enthusiasm at the prospect of playing doggie outside of the fence, with real doggies wandering around.

"Um, no honey. We're almost home. You can use our toilet."

"Why don't you tell the man he can use our toilet?"

Good question. "Because he doesn't live at our house. He's a stranger."

"Where does he live, mommy?"

I look at the man more closely. Having just peed in the middle of a road in broad daylight, taking no measures to even attempt to conceal the activity from the many people milling about, I expect to see a haggard and downtrodden person in rags stumbling along until the need to lay down and take a nap takes over.

But actually, this man is clean. No dirt streaks on his face, no visible rips in his clothes. Ok, he's wearing a white T-shirt that said "Curves" in pink letters, meaning that his shirt is probably second hand (unless, of course, he works out at this American gym for full-figured women), but he is also wearing sturdy shoes and he looks like he is headed somewhere with a purpose instead of aimlessly roaming the neighborhood.

"I have absolutely no idea where he lives." Maybe a big house, maybe a shack, maybe the street. There is no way for me to tell. This revelation hits me hard because suddenly it is extremely apparent how very disconnected I am, and will continue to be, from my surroundings. I am at a loss at how to process all that I see, and recognize that I am completely out of my league. The realization is demoralizing.

I had started my stroll hoping to somehow connect with my neighborhood on some level - that because we have the commonality of living together in the same place, and because I came to this country with the intent to help in some small way - I could find common ground with my neighbors. Yet the looks of those I passed as I strolled along the dirt road seemed to imply that my presence was somehow offensive to them. I had the disconcerting feeling that the mere fact that as a foreigner - as an outsider mingling out in the open, outside the walls of my big fancy house, outside of my big, fancy car - I was somehow flaunting my good fortune and my advantages at their expense. I dejectedly concluded that my presence is not welcome as I turned the corner toward home.

Sullen and deep in thought, I am taken by surprise by the sudden appearance of a woman who somehow materializes directly in front of me with her hands out, palms up. Her eyes are covered over in a milky-white film, her exposed flesh full of sores. She emits a moaning sound as she moves her hands every-so-slightly up and down to indicate she's asking for money.

Once initiated, everyone wants money and a kind of slow motion, mini-swarm ensues. Still trying to recover from the vision of the woman's pitiful state as I make deliberate progress toward my home's gate despite the growing mass of people now trailing me, a tall, powerfully-built, well-groomed man dressed in jeans and a black polo shirt angrily pushes away the small mob. Blocking my path entirely, he asserts he is a refugee from Darfur and aggressively demands money.

"You give money. Now."

I ignore him, staring blankly but intently at my home's gate just up ahead as I try to walk purposefully in the direction of my home.

"I refugee Darfur. I REFUGEE. You money. NOW."

Persisting with his loud, monosyllabic demands, I start to panic. While somehow managing to make steady progress toward gate, I nervously mutter, "I have no money with me. I only just want to walk with my children outside." Am I in the process of being mugged in broad daylight?

The irate man lets out a disgusted grunt and begins wildly gesticulating, loudly ranting in a language I can't understand as he storms off in the opposite direction from me.

Relieved, I make a frantic dash with the stroller to my compound and I slam the gate shut behind me. Leaning against the gate's thick metal carriage while struggling to catch my breath, my heart beating out of control, I sadly resign myself to join the rest of the expatriate foreigners I have met and learn to accept Ethiopia's ubiquitous 10-foot walls that close me in. I tried, but it seems there is no sense fighting it - the world outside these fences is a tough and unpredictable place for which my sheltered life and limited experiences have not adequately prepared me.

Reflecting on this lesson three years later and at the end of my time in Ethiopia, perhaps that supposed Darfur refugee really did steal from me that day. Not money or possessions. Instead, he robbed me of my naiveté. He took my smile.

CHAPTER 9
The Party – Eleven O'Clock
Food is Plenty, Glass is Full or Empty?

Eleven o'clock has finally arrived, and the rest of my guests are due to show up shortly. All is good. I have plenty of food that looks and smells perfect. I have a huge bouncy castle up and running, with three ecstatic little girls jumping their hearts out. Fasika and Tigist are working with me hand-in-hand to take care of all the finishing touches, and my rock of a husband is somehow managing to pull himself together after his harrowing encounter on the Ring Road. As Fasika, Tigist, and I are setting out the food on an outdoor buffet table, Brian yells out to Fasika to ask if she brought any music.

"Hey Fasika – I need a little help here to get in the party mood. Did you bring some of your CD's?"

Fasika hands me a plate full of injera and tells me to stack the spongy, sour dough-flavored pancake-like bread that is a traditional staple in the Ethiopian diet. "Make like this," she says, indicating I should roll up the injera in spirals and stack the rolls in a pyramid shape.

"Yes ma'am," I say with a salute. She smiles as she walks toward the back of our compound, to the room she keeps between the garage and the walk-in food pantry. She returns a couple minutes later with a towering stack of Ethiopian music.

"Ok, which one Mr. Brian?"

"Are those all Ethiopian CDs?"

She laughs. "I have too many. I have many more my home. Too many good Ethiopia singers. You choose."

Brian has no idea. To us, the music all sounds so much alike. At the same time, though, I've never heard anything like it. Ethiopian music is clearly different from anything else you'll encounter anywhere in the world. Like their food, traditional dress, their Ethiopian Orthodox calendar that has them several years behind the Western calendar, their unique way of telling time that is six hours off from the rest of the world (noon is six o'clock Ethiopian time), the music hails from a place that only exists in this country. Because of Ethiopia's remote and often inhospitable and inaccessible landscape, the area known as Abyssinia existed and developed its civilization and society in virtual isolation, essentially cut off from the world and all of its influences well into the late 1800s. The people of modern-day Ethiopia, products of this deeply insular and isolated history, are intensely proud of their unique culture. And they hold their music in very high regard.

Brian knows this and is aware that he cannot offend. Fasika in particular is fiercely defensive of her culture. He sifts through Fasika's stack with a look of great consternation and finally chooses one with a beautiful Ethiopian woman on the cover. "This one's my favorite," he says, holding the CD up for Fasika to see before taking it over to the CD player. "Actually, can I upload some of these to my iPod so that we can use the iPod stereo for the party instead of dealing with all these extension cords to get the CD player and speakers outside? Also, that means I can have some of the music to take with me back to America."

Fasika goes flush with pride. "Yes, please take to add to your i-machine radio. You enjoy and show to others our great Ethiopia songs."

As Brian goes inside to try to transfer Fasika's music to the iPod, my cell phone rings. It's Tesfaye the Optimist. He's calling to apologize for being late (it's only 11:05), but he's just around the corner.

"No worries Tesfaye. Fasika, Tigist and Blen are here. They came early to help. You'll likely be the first of the large group of guests to arrive." But Tesfaye worries. Punctuality is very important to him.

"Well, because we're talking, can I ask if you are free for tomorrow night? I know you leave very soon, but there is something very important. Your help could be nice."

Tesfaye is very active. Whether in his studies, in various jobs with non-governmental organizations and agencies, start-up business opportunities, with church, or volunteer charity groups, he's always on the go. Always looking for a new way to make a difference, to help, even if only in some small way.

The human spirit is an amazing thing, and Tesfaye is the embodiment of the endurance of those special few who refuse to become demoralized by their circumstances or indifferent to their surroundings. Despite all the obstacles that Ethiopia erects to stifle development, in spite of all the unnecessary hardships inflicted on the ordinary citizenry and the plethora of inhumane conditions that confront the abject poor, people like Tesfaye continue to toil within the confines of their system with the hopes of making Ethiopia a slightly better place to call home.

"What is it this time?"

Tesfaye explains that he recently discovered this great group of volunteers who work with vulnerable youths to provide them vocational training as an alternative to begging. Tesfaye says that tomorrow he organized a soccer match for the youths and has planned an Ethiopian-style soup kitchen for after the game. The youth players will be eating, but also helping to serve others.

"But we need more volunteers to help deliver the food to the people. Always too many hungry people. Can you help with us to give the food?"

"Sure, but only if I can come early and watch the game."

"Yes, yes! And we can talk about the new things with my farmer project." Tesfaye is working with an international aid organization to help rural farmers adapt to climate change. "I have big news. Very exciting. But not now. I tell you when I come to you. I want to see your face to see your happiness with the progress."

Tesfaye's enthusiasm, energy, and drive to help rural Ethiopian farmers combat food insecurity and poverty is unflappable. From the first day I met him for coffee over two years ago, he has demonstrated an unyielding devotion to this cause, and even managed to crack a bit of my hardening, cynical shell in the process.

"Ok, I'll wait, but come soon."

"Yes, yes. I think three minutes. I see the corner of the goats now. I walk left with the goats, yes?"

"Yes, turn left at the goats."

I hang up my cell phone and there's a knock at the door. A whole group arrives together as Fasika opens the gate. It's my driver Shibru and his wife and their five kids coming through the gate door. I wave and shout hello, making my way over to the door.

As we all say our greetings, Shibrus' kids' eyes are glued to the bouncy castle, their expressions as if they just walked into Santa's toy workshop at the North Pole. I motion to the kids to knock themselves at the bouncy castle. They tentatively look at me, then at their dad with hope in their eyes. Dad shakes his head yes, the kids look back at me with giant smiles, and off all five of them go. The whole exchange took less than a minute.

"We won't be seeing any of them today," I joke, happy that the castle is in for quite a work out. Shibru smiles and politely offers a muffled, nervous laugh. He doesn't understand a word I say. But just as I'm about to call over Fasika to join our group and help with translation to overcome our awkward silence, I feel a tap on my shoulder.

"Kiiirrrrsteeen!" I turn and see that somehow my Ethiopian sunshine managed to arrive through the gate without me noticing.

"Tesfaye! Welcome!"

"Kirsten — let me tell you all that has happened," he says with contained excitement, guiding me toward one of our outdoor wicker chairs with an air of secretive confidence, his tone and body language a unique a mixture of playful intensity and dire importance. "We are making big changes!"

CHAPTER 10

Tesfaye – The Gods Must Be Angry

"When it is dark enough, you can see the stars."
- Ralph Waldo Emerson

Imagine that you're a farmer. Not a dairy farmer from Vermont whose cows lounge all day on custom-made water beds to reduce their stress levels so they can produce a better quality of milk. No, you're a subsistence farmer living in rural Ethiopia, eking out a meager existence from your small plot of infertile land. You live in a one room

hut with a thatched roof and a dirt floor, lucky to have
shelter during the big rains. You don't know your age. You
have ten children, although two died before the age of five.
You've never been to school. You eat when there is food.
If the rains are good, you eat. If they're very good, you eat
and sell a surplus for much needed cash. If the rains are
bad, you're hungry. And it all depends on the whims of the
gods.

Approximately 85% of Ethiopia's 77 million people
are small-scale subsistence farmers dependent upon rain-
fed agriculture. In a country renowned for chronic
malnutrition and food insecurity, changing rain patterns
associated with climate variability represent real dangers to
much of Ethiopia.

I ponder these facts as I'm sitting in an Addis Ababa
café, waiting to meet a young Ethiopian environmental
activist who is interested in discussing climate change
implications for Ethiopia with someone from the United
States. My table wobbles on its faulty legs as I lean forward
to try and catch a waiter's attention. It's my third attempt,
and this time I'm able to make eye contact that he can't
ignore. The waiter ambles over to my table and I ask for a
double macchiato. It is one of the pure joys of living in
Ethiopia. The strong, bitter, robust coffee prepared Italian-
style is my hopeless vice.

Enraptured in a state of aromatic coffee bliss, I don't see Tesfaye as he enters the café. In fact, I jump a little at his sudden appearance in the chair opposite me, but he is equally off balance at seeing me settled into my seat with a half-empty cup of coffee.

"I am late?" He glances at his watch in a near panic. "No, it is 3:00. I am punctual. Very punctual."

It is obviously important to him that I acknowledge that he arrived at his meeting with me on time. "Yes, perfectly punctual. It was me that arrived early. Um, there was much less traffic than I had expected," I added almost apologetically.

"No problem. We can talk now."

Tesfaye is in his mid-twenties and is well dressed, he has a gleaming white smile that he's not afraid to flash, and he's clearly driven by the need to establish himself as a respectable professional of Western standards. He is punctual. That is clear. He also wants to get down to business quickly, because he is a busy man. He starts our meeting off with a rundown of his credentials.

"It is very nice to meet the U.S. Embassy. I am an anthropologist. I delivered my master's thesis at Kyoto in Japan. I want a PhD, but this will take three or four years. Kyoto has a scholarship to sponsor me, but I don't know.

Maybe I prefer the UK or U.S. because this is English and I can work. Things are very expensive. Maybe I will stay here and make a difference."

I take advantage of a pause in his rapid-fire introduction, breaking in with, "Very impressive, Tesfaye. I wish you luck in all your big decisions. It's great that you have so many options. Now, you had mentioned that you work with a non-governmental organization that focuses on the environment. Can you tell me about some of your environmental outreach activities?" I ask, trying to steer the conversation toward my objectives.

"Yes, yes. You know, climate change is a big problem for us. In Ethiopia. In Africa. We are vulnerable. Our farmers are suffering. They do not understand."

"What do you mean when you say they do not understand?"

"Well, my organization, we made a survey study. Here in Ethiopia. We asked farmers if the rains are changed. We asked if they know why the rains changed. We also asked if they changed their farming ways. You know, to adapt."

"And?" I'm hanging on his words.

"Well, most all said yes to rain changes. Maybe 80% said the rain problems are because the gods are angry," he adds, his nervous eyes giving away a tinge of embarrassment.

"And what about adaptation measures?"

"Well, they say they need to make the gods happy again. This can mean more animal sacrifices. Maybe they sin too much and need to change behavior. Not so much alcohol, you know. Many times they shrug and say - it is God's will, so what can I do if he wants me to suffer?"

"Oh." I stall for time, to collect my thoughts. "So, what is the next step for your organization now that you have this revealing information from your study?"

"We will start an education program in these areas. It is important to give them information. Many do not have school, so how can they know?"

"True, true." I ponder the practicalities. "But will this rural, largely uneducated audience be able to make the intellectual leap from angry gods to carbon emission particles gathering in our Earth's atmosphere in greater numbers due to increases in industrial outputs worldwide?" I try not to sound sarcastic.

"You are right. They cannot. That is why we are focused on the religious leaders. They can transmit messages and the people will trust them."

"Good point." Again, call me cynical, but my pragmatic brain flashes more red flags. "But are these leaders receptive to the idea that they should inform their followers that changes in rainfall are not due to the gods from which they derive their power, but due to scientific factors out of their control?"

"Yes, well, they support us. We have religious men, the important ones, looking through the Bible and other religious books to find words that say you must protect the environment. The leaders are speeding to find the most words first. They tell their people, 'you must protect the environment. See here, the Bible says to. If you do not, you will be punished. The rains will change.' They are finding more words every day. We have big hopes that the people will listen." At this point, Tesfaye is twitching with excitement in his rickety plastic chair. Still, I have to keep pushing.

"Is that fair? Becoming a good steward of your environment is an important lesson to instill and promoting this premise is necessary and laudable, but is it ethical to imply that changing rain patterns will then stabilize?"

Tesfaye's enthusiasm drains from his face, his expression transforming to something more grim and determined. "Our people have no education. We must help them. We tell them, 'Do not cut down all the trees.' We tell them the animals should not pollute the water they use. We say 'you should not pollute the water with your waste.' We tell them these things, but they do not listen. They do not understand why these things are bad, how these things hurt their lives. We must find new ways to change them. Maybe this way will work. I think yes. It is the good way. Then, I hope the West can find a way to help with the rains." With that, he glances down at his watch.

Tesfaye had told me when we arranged the meeting that he only had 30 minutes to spend with me and then he had to be off to another meeting. He explained that he is trying to start a business from his home - he had recently bought a large washing machine for clothes so that he can charge people by the kilo to use it. A budding entrepreneur in addition to being an energetic environmental activist and potential PhD scholar. Tesfaye certainly is an impressive, and punctual, young man. I try to help him make an easy exit.

"Ok, I was a skeptic, but maybe you have converted me to your plan. It was a real pleasure to talk to you today and hear your unique insights. Thank you very much for sharing. I wish you the best of luck, with your work in Ethiopia and on making your decisions for your future.

Please, let's stay in touch."

"Thank you also. It was kind to talk to you about these passions. I hope to talk again," he says, shaking my hand goodbye.

"As do I," I reply, realizing with slight surprise that my auto-pilot response is truly genuine. And reflecting on my conversation with Tesfaye after he leaves, taking in the last drops of my delicious coffee alone at my wobbly plastic table, I chuckle at this latest round of absurdity that has just been flung my way. In sum, Tesfaye's main objective is to move from "the gods are very angry, so we need more animal sacrifices, we need to stop sinning, and/or what can we do if it's the gods will that we suffer," to "the gods are very angry, so we need to stop pooping in our water." Is this really progress?

At the end of the day, I think yes. Rainfall will continue to vary but, according to Tesfaye's plan, maybe this can be used as a catalyst to improve water supply sanitation and hygiene in Ethiopia while the rest of the world continues to debate and negotiate an international climate change strategy. That is progress. It is "the good way." Is this fair, is it ethical? Tesfaye would argue, - who cares, because if it works, then it makes life a little better. And life needs to get better.

CHAPTER 11
The Party – Twelve O'Clock
My Driver is a Lawyer,
Will You Be My Pharmacist?

It's noon. The sun is shining, the music is blaring, food is flowing, the bouncy castle is bouncing - my party full of Ethiopian friends is in full swing. I'm happily enjoying my conversation with Tesfaye, amazed by his energy and enthusiasm, when Fasika approaches me with my cell phone.

"It rings."

"Ok, thanks," I say taking the phone from her. "Hello?" It's Mohammed, Fatima's husband. "Sorry to call. I couldn't reach Brian." His normally ultra-calm, slightly Arabic-accented voice is rushed and disjointed."

"What's wrong?"

"It's Fatima. She was at her spinning class today and her pedal fell off. She came crashing down onto the bicycle seat which wasn't cushioned. We went to the Korean hospital and had x-rays- they

think she broke her tailbone. They want to give Fatima some anesthesia even though she's allergic, so we left before they did any terrible damage. She's in so much pain. I'm trying to get her on a flight to Egypt, it looks like we'll get one tonight at two or three in the morning. But she's in so much pain."

Fatima is the dynamic wife of my Egyptian diplomat colleague. Not content with being a stay home wife and mom, but unable to work in Ethiopia because of her diplomat spouse status, she's started a purse design business and also volunteered to be a spinning class instructor at a local gym in exchange for free use of the equipment.

In no time, Fatima developed quite a following and had to expand her number of classes. The gym benefited immensely, but you wouldn't know it with the equipment seriously deteriorating over time. Fatima warned the management and owners several times that the bikes were becoming unsafe and needed to be serviced. Her advice went unheeded. Instead, it was generally met with 'what can we do' shrugs. The owners were making good money, there was a large membership pool, so why waste all these wonderful profits on something like maintenance?

"I have some of my painkiller medicine left over from when I needed that root canal a few months ago. If it doesn't help, it will at least knock her out so she can sleep through the pain. Massive ibuprofen dose with some codeine, but there's only a couple pills left."

Some months back, my mouth exploded in pain. I saw the embassy health unit doctor who put me on the next plane for Nairobi to get an emergency root canal. With no dentists in Ethiopia operating at international standards, the closest dentist appointment destination was Kenya, and the next flight wasn't leaving for another ten hours. The embassy doctor mercifully gave me the pain killers.

"Oh, Kirsten, that would be great. We don't have anything strong enough here at our house. Can I send my driver now to pick up the pills?"

Generally, we don't use local pharmacies, being advised that they sell expired medications with tampered expiration dates, tampered medicines, the wrong medicines, Chinese manufactured pirated medicines, and so on. Instead, we plan ahead and order as much as we can to keep our medicine cabinets stocked with whatever might be needed. And when that fails, the American diplomats are lucky enough to have the Embassy health unit.

"Sure. I'll have it ready when your driver Girma arrives. I'm here all day." Just then, there's a burst of loud laughter from the kids inside the bouncy castle.

"Oh - your party. I forgot. I'm so sorry to interrupt."

"Mohammed, no worries. You've got bigger problems to deal with than having Girma crash my party for five minutes. All my best to Fatima. I hope the pills help."

This is the fourth time this week I've been asked for medicine.

Fasika came to work with a headache, so I gave her a couple of Excedrin. Tigist had a stuffy nose and cough, so daytime Sudafed did the trick. When Shibru arrived at work limping, his face screwed up in pain, I didn't know what to do. Fasika said, "His leg has pain. It is cold. He went to the hospital and they gave him a shot for cold leg and told him to keep his leg warm."

This was more than I could handle with my amateur home pharmacy, so I sent Shibru to see my friend's Ethiopian-Greek acupuncturist with a sealed envelope full of money. Poor Shibru didn't know what he was in for, but the pins apparently worked and he returned to work the next day with a smile and said to me, "Me good now. You like mama."

And what a relief. In fact, my Egyptian friend Fatima had just told me a story about hoe her friend's housekeeper's mother had visited a hospital because of a numbing feeling in her hands that seemed to be spreading. Based on the description, Fatima said the mother was likely experiencing the onset of multiple sclerosis. The hospital, however, felt otherwise and said she was cold and needed a shot near her spine, probably some type of steroid to reduce swelling.

In no time, the mother was unable to walk. Fatima advised her friend to pay for the mother to visit this miracle worker, Roberto the Ethio-Greek acupuncturist, to see what could be done. Roberto examined her and said she was paralyzed. The shot had somehow damaged her spinal cord and there was nothing even magical Roberto could do for her.

So when Shibru returned from Roberto - a smiling, English speaking man, with two good legs - I was thrilled. Shibru supports a wife and five kids who all sleep in the same bed in their three-room dwelling on the outskirts of Addis. Under these conditions, if Shibru were to lose the ability to work because of a bad leg or any other health-related reason that can occur at any time, his entire family would be in jeopardy. There's no unemployment insurance, there's no welfare check. Only hunger and homelessness. I wonder if this is the story of so many of the deformed beggars that wander the streets of Addis Ababa —once regular, kind, and hard-working people, until disaster strikes and leaves you destitute.

A honk outside my gate pulls me from lapsing back into melancholy thoughts about these good people's hardships. The horn is from Fatima's driver Girma – he has arrived to pick up the medication and Shibru is already opening the gate so the car can pull into our driveway.

"Hi Girma."

"Hello ma'am." He looks longingly at the yard filled with all kinds of party paraphernalia, smiles and laughter filling the air, food heaped high on plates.

"Sorry Girma, I didn't yet have a chance to get the pills. Let me go inside and run upstairs. Please, help yourself to some food. The plates are over there," I say pointing to the far end of the buffet table. He accepts with a grateful smile and begins walking toward the food.

When I come back outside, I see Girma in the middle of the crowd, eating and laughing with the others. I look from him to the stack of "gifts" I've piled to the side of our house, and contemplate adding Girma to my list of give-away recipients today.

The gift pile has become a quarterly ritual Brian and I instituted as a way to deal with the guilt of having so much. Every three months Brian, the kids, and I scour the house on a clutter purging mission. We pile the masses of unneeded items into a corner, separate them out, and give them away to the staff, which they gladly accept. Not just clothes and toys - they are happy to take everything, from empty Christmas cookie tins (they make for good food storage) to broken coffee makers (it makes a useful pitcher) and a burned-out motor from a blow up bed (the electrical cord with copper wires can fetch a high price at the local markets).

Yes, there's more than enough for all today. I pick up a small pile and call Girma over.

"Here you go, the pills for Fatima. I wish you could stay, but I know Fatima needs you today." He nods his head. "How about taking these things with you? Since we're leaving Ethiopia next weekend, there's so much that we just don't have room to take with us."

"Yes, thank you. Thank you very much. Very kind. I will take." He pauses. "I know you leave soon. I know you kind person. Maybe you know someone who needs driver? My cousin, he needs work. Maybe you know?"

I've met Girma's cousin a couple of times. He used to work for a diplomat friend who was with a Scandinavian Embassy, but that diplomat left Ethiopia two months ago and apparently the cousin hadn't yet found new employment. Both Girma and his cousin studied law together at Addis Ababa University, yet they struggle to stay employed as drivers with expatriate families.

"Well, I can't think of anyone, but I'll talk to people at our Embassy on Monday and do my best. If I find someone, I'll be in touch with Fatima."

"Thank you ma'am. He needs the help. No work is hard now. Prices keep rising. Food is too much money."

"I know. Here." *I heap another spoonful of food onto a paper plate.* "Take this with you." *It's not much, but it's what can I do at the moment.*

Girma gets back into Fatima's car and starts to back out of the driveway. I see Shibru making his way to the gate, so I run to get there first, shouting to him, "No, Shibru, I will get the gate. Today the party is for you! Go back, eat more, dance more, enjoy more!" *Shibru looks at me with a confused expression, but then smiles and walks back towards his wife who's standing in the middle of my large crowd of guests.*

I close the gate behind Girma as he drives off to bring Fatima her much needed pain killers. Standing there with my back to the closed gate, gazing in the direction of the happy party crowd, I take a minute to wonder what my guests would be doing if they were free to pursue their dreams. Fasika longs to own a beauty salon and she would undoubtedly be a successful business woman. Tigist talks of how she would like to work as a nanny one day because of her love for children, although I think she would make a wonderful primary school teacher. Tesfaye should be a tycoon — the altruistic kind who redirects his fortune to meet philanthropic goals. And Shibru is such a gentle and kind man, I imagine him contributing to society by working to help people in some way, maybe a social worker.

But this is all moot. These trustworthy, hardworking people are primarily household staff to foreign expatriate families because these are the jobs they can access and the salaries are good. And they will tell you they are lucky. Maybe they can't climb social or professional ladders, maybe they are not free to choose whether or not they marry, maybe they don't really own their future or know what tomorrow will bring. But they say it is a good life.

Even Shibru says he feels lucky to work as a day guard/gardener at my home while he and his family live in a three-room dwelling on the edge of town, in a place where they have no running water and only sporadic electricity, and they routinely confiscate discarded items they find in my home. How could this be lucky? Shibru answers that he feels lucky because he says he is not poor. In Ethiopia, somehow, this is not poor.

CHAPTER 12

Shibru – Climbing Ladders without Hands

"Can a man who is warm understand one who is freezing?"
– Alexander Solzhenitsyn

My four-year old daughter climbed to the top of a heap of gravel in the middle of a small yard strewn with discarded animal parts. There are no toys to be found, so she searches the mound for random items of interest: oddly shaped stones, sticks, a chicken's foot. Roosters and hens mill in and out of their hutches, occasionally chased by stray dogs wandering in through gaps in the corrugated tin fence that partially encloses this small compound. Glassy-eyed children roam around, letting the many flies land on their faces and bodies unmolested.

Within thirty minutes of arrival at my gardener Shibru's home on the outskirts of Addis Ababa, Ethiopia - here to celebrate Shibru's youngest son's birthday - my entire body feels encrusted in dirt, it seeping into my every orifice as a light breeze kicks up new waves of the powdery dust.

The house at the far end of the small enclosure is a three-room structure. The home is still under construction and has burlap fabric for a door separating the common room from what must be the one bedroom. There is only one electrical fixture in sight, a single naked bulb dangling from the ceiling in the center of the windowless common room. The bulb is off despite the indoor darkness, and there doesn't appear to be a bathroom or running water in the house. The walls are bare except for a few pictures of Jesus and Mary and some hanging rotary beads, a reflection of Ethiopia's strong Orthodox Christian heritage. A predominantly Orthodox Christian country, this home is particularly religious. Sunday services are mandatory and alcohol is prohibited.

Sitting in the small, dark dwelling in overstuffed, mismatched chairs that line the periphery of the rectangular room with its rough, concrete floor, I am among ten or so guests. Shibru's blind father, the patriarch of this large family that consists of two wives and fourteen children, many grandchildren, cousins, and so forth, is tucked away in the room's back corner, flinging his horse hair fly swatter at phantom flies as he hums a random tune. Aside from his intermittent murmurings, the room is largely silent; the party guests either staring straight ahead or speaking quietly to the person seated next to them.

Although transfixed by the image of the blind father, my eyes eventually begin to wander. I soon notice that the rooms' small, corner shelves are filled with my home's discarded plastic margarita mix bottles – a staple in our home, but severely out of place here. The bottles are now being used to store our old *Conde Nast Travel* and *Money* magazines, among a multitude of other uses.

Once I notice the bottles and magazines, it is as if all of our discarded "trash" starts popping out of the mud work. In no time, I see a pile of our discarded books sitting prominently in a neat pile directly below portraits of Jesus and Mary.

Yes, I had recently thrown away a few books from our home. Of course, one should never throw away books, but these three happen to be an exception to the rule.

The first book now in Shibru's pile is *Lets Go Thailand*, a 1991 version. For anyone planning to travel to Thailand, I don't recommend reviewing the best places as discovered by Harvard students in 1991. It just doesn't seem useful. The second book is an analysis of the Maastricht Treaty from the mid-1980s. Definitely outdated. Both had been easy trash can decisions.

As for the third book - the one placed at the top of the pile just under the portrait of the Virgin Mary and flanked by empty margarita mix bottles - is entitled, *The Ultimate Guide to Felatio*. No need for details on that one. Suffice it to say I had tired of hiding the book and eventually decided to say my farewell. So off to the bin it went before, unbeknownst to me, finding its final pious resting place in Shibru's home.

Humorous irony aside, having uncovered Ethiopia's stealthy recycling industry, I am now very careful about what I throw away. Instead of casually tossing out plastic or glass bottles, I now set them aside on the counter for the taking. I never throw out old magazines, having learned that these glossy English reading materials are used as coveted display items, so they too get placed in a pile for removal. Unmentionables of whatever form are now discreetly hidden, buried beneath mounds of trash to ensure against another immaculate reincarnation.

A less humorous revelation during this visit is that Shibru's household, despite the austere conditions, is not poor. By Ethiopian standards, Shibru and his extended family are Ethiopia's equivalent of the broad middle class. They are furniture makers and shop keepers, some of which are educated and professional. They are hardworking people who are deeply proud of their country and their culture. Yet they are representative of Ethiopia's segment of society who are not from the leading party's tribe and therefore lack vital political connections. As such, they are significantly hindered from moving up society's ladder in a meaningful way despite all the potential they represent for their country. Instead, they plod along in life, doing what they can and taking pride in what they have.

It's a lot to take in. After a mere two hours, I am physically and mentally exhausted as I say my goodbyes to this birthday gathering, with a certain relief.

Although I'm now in a rush to get to a local restaurant to meet a friend for lunch, I find myself facing one of those moments where I wish I had the time and ability to just "go blank." To discard thoughts about life's unfairness and the powers of chance that led to me being born American. But there's no time. So, with my two kids strapped into their car seats, I brave the chaotic capital city's roads and head off to meet my friend across town. It's not easy. Immediately upon starting the drive, Alexandra starts in on her vomit monologues.

Moving to Ethiopia, your stomach has to adjust to the new and different types of bacteria it will encounter. And, given poor hygienic standards, your stomach often endures far more than it's ever been conditioned to face. My iron-stomach husband, who never took a sick day during his entire school life, has been knocked out flat several times from gastro-intestinal "setbacks."

Being from more sickly stock, I try to avoid food except for what is cooked at home in my kitchen by Tigist, confident that she will soak everything in a bacteria-killing bleach solution. But despite my diligent precautions, I've also suffered the violent bouts of angry stomach vomiting and on too many occasions had to return home to change clothes because of a close encounter of the "number two" kind.

Lauren, after recently succeeding in the potty training stage, got a particular kick out of witnessing one of my attacks, chanting "mommy poo-poos in her pants," repeatedly to all her little preschool cohorts. Not wanting to be outdone by her older sister, Alexandra created the game of fake vomiting for attention and now spends car rides imitating vomit sounds for our listening entertainment. "Mommy, this is a vomit: Auurrggh. Mommy, this is a cow vomit: Auuurrggh. Mommy, this is a sheep vomit: Auurrggh." And so on.

In no time, to the background noise of Alexandra's vomit reenactments, I encounter a four way intersection where eight lanes of traffic converge into one "X" without the assistance of a traffic light. The key to navigating these intersection death traps is to appear strong and fearless - no matter what is barreling at you head on, it is incumbent upon you to edge out your opponents and stake your position on the road, heading straight into the intersection, swerving as necessary, always moving somewhat forward. Easier said than done, but I somehow manage to conquer this zero-sum game and win the battle of wills.

Next challenge? The cow stampede. Being that today is slaughter day in Addis Ababa, I watch in horror as a massive herd of long-horned cows, ribs protruding from their bloated bellies, come barreling headlong toward me and the rest of the oncoming traffic before a lone, teenage shepherd is able to somehow exercise control over the mayhem and contain the stampede. Continuing on, I manage to survive a "flash before your eyes" moment when a person juts out right in front of my car from some invisible starting point. Swerving in a panic, I miss the pedestrian by mere inches just before thankfully reaching the restaurant where I am to meet my friend.

But my friend isn't at the restaurant when I arrive. She calls a few minutes later to say she is running slightly late - traffic. Her voice sounds frazzled, frustrated, and very agitated. I commiserate, picturing the cows, goats, and donkeys; the endless waves of pedestrians choking up the roads; and the intersection traffic jams where the game of chicken sometimes goes awry.

Sitting at the restaurant table as I wait for my friend, sipping on a glass of sparkling water with my two exhausted toddlers thankfully asleep in their double stroller, I find myself gazing absent mindedly out the restaurant's smudged window at a group of stray dogs busily chasing after a bloodied animal skull. Overtaken by a homesick haze, my mind slowly drifts back to my college days in Charleston, SC; to the carefree times spent watching my dog, Wendyll, run up and down Charleston's barrier island beaches, exuberantly chasing seagulls in an endless pursuit of pure bliss.

଄ଌ଄ଌ

After losing my family dog Boe to cancer while I was in college, I never expected to get another dog. Boe was one of the special creatures that can never be replaced. But the hole he left behind, while healing, wasn't closing. Eventually I decided that finding a new dog would not be disloyal to Boe's memory, but would be a way to carry on the love I had for Boe through another pet. In some ways, continuing to love a dog is a way of paying tribute to those you've loved and lost. At least that's how I looked at it as I tried to justify searching the classifieds.

On the first day of my search, I saw a listing for free puppies that lived on a horse farm just outside of town. Because most dog lovers have a preconceived notion of what a dog is, and should be, based on their childhood experience, my free dog had to be a male, black and tan mutt. I called the number listed in the ad and asked if they still had puppies. Yuuus, came the heavily accented, Southern-drawl reply. Did they have any boys? Yuuuus. Did they have a black and tan boy? Yuuuuus. They had one. The rest were black with the odd white spot.

Oh no, those would just not do. I launched into a desperate plea with the woman to have her save the black and tan for me – I was on my way.

I arrived at the farm as quickly as my third-hand, banged up Ford Escort could take me, ran out of my car without even bothering to close the door, and sprinted up to the house. Frantically banging on the screen door, a large woman eventually came sauntering toward me from the kitchen.

"What's burnin' your butt?"

Huh? "Um, is this the place with the puppies?"

"Puppies? Oh – that litter of mutts is out back. I think they're havin' their grits now. Come on, have a look."

Please let the black and tan still be there, please let the black and tan still be there, please let the black and tan still be there, I desperately repeated to myself as if in prayer.

We walked through the house, out the back porch, and into the yard. Sure enough, a whole litter of 8-week old puppies was chowing down on a communal bowl of grits. From the looks of it, there hadn't been a mad rush to take these puppies home, and my little black and tan guy was happily eating his dinner with his siblings.

"You like horses?" The woman asked to break the silence as I stared at the adorable tufts of round-bellied puppy fur balls positioning themselves with their oversized paws to vie for the optimal grits consumption spot. I shook my head yes to affirm that I like horses, but the puppy cuteness factor was in overdrive and I was rendered speechless.

"Well, come on down and I'll show you what we got here. It'll give the little varmints time to finish supper."

So off we walked down through an overgrown field littered with rusting farm equipment to a small stable. Guess who should stop eating that delicious meal of grits to come along on our mini trek, but little mister black and tan. It was destiny. The woman told me she had been calling him Bear or Wendel, but he didn't know his name yet so I was free to choose something new.

Wendel! What a perfect name for a little southern dog. My ecstatic reaction stemmed from the fact that two of my college friends who had grown up together in a suburb of Charleston had had a neighborhood friend named Wendel during their elementary school years. The three of them were constantly causing trouble and no matter what, the stories ended with "and it was all Wendel's fault." Easy to blame Wendel since he eventually moved away and was no longer around to defend himself.

I came to love what I had deemed the "Wendel stories" described in typical southern fashion using phrases like "he was busier than a one-legged man at a butt kicking contest" and I would always ask my two friends for more. The fact that this adorable, goofy little butter ball southern puppy rolling around my feet was called Wendel was just too perfect. In fact, he was so perfect that I decided on a unique spelling, Wendyll – my idyllic puppy. I scooped him up, gave him a big squeeze, took him home, and never stopped hugging him.

Wendyll was simply the greatest dog. He was intelligent, easy to train, sweet, loyal, fun, easy going, and adorable. Unconditional love flowed from both of us and I spent every available moment with him. The only unavoidable separation was when I was in class, and that was painful.

In time, my friends began to get annoyed by my absence from college social life and one evening came to my apartment en-mass for what they deemed to be an "intervention." They told me I was going to go out for the night. I was not permitted to go home before midnight and only allowed to mention or make reference to Wendyll one time. Torture. How could it be done? Just short of putting a bag over my head and dragging me out of the house, they did somehow manage to get me to abandon my puppy for that evening.

To avoid future interventions, I eventually settled into a compromise routine where I would see friends at events that allowed dogs or invite people to my beach house apartment for a day at the ocean. On one occasion, soon after college graduation, my friend and her new husband had just bought their first home. They were having a house warming party and invited me. I said yes, but that I'd have to bring Wendyll if that was ok. My friend hesitantly replied that it would be fine as long as he was housebroken and I assured her that of course perfect little Wendyll never had accidents.

About thirty minutes into the party, my panicked home-owner friend pointed to Wendyll, shouting, "Hey – what's he doing?"

I looked. Oh no. Wendyll was in full squatting position in the middle of their brand new white rug. No time to think - must act fast.

I grabbed an old sock toy I had brought with me and held it right below his butt, catching the poo as it trailed out of him in a long, flowing strand. Feeling quite proud that my quick thinking had saved the day, or at least the rug, I looked up from my dog's butt, sock poo in hand, with a big, satisfied grin. But to my surprise, my smile was met by a room full of disgusted, even mortified, faces.

"Is lunch ready yet?" was the only thing I could think to say.

A couple of months passed with a few more "accidents," the expected number of shoes and miscellaneous leather items destroyed, a few more interventions, and soon it was time to move to Washington, DC, followed by Paris, France, to begin my career as a diplomat, Wendyll at my side every step of the way.

From train rides traversing the bucolic European countryside, to exploring the spectacular Chateau region of the Loire Valley, wandering through the rustic pastoral country lanes of Bordeaux, discovering Monet's dramatic coastal cliffs of *Etretat* that overhang a turbulent sea, and happily strolling through Paris' Rive Gauche district

bursting with quaint sidewalk cafes - Wendyll and I
certainly led an idyllic life together.

Reflecting on the movement of time, missing my
precious dog as I gazed out the restaurant's grimy window
in Ethiopia while waiting for my friend to arrive at this
restaurant, a loud door slam startles me out of my
daydream. I look up at the entrance to see my friend come
storming into the restaurant in a huff. She slams her purse
down on our table, looks at me and loudly blurts out, "If
one more person treats me like an ATM or grocery store,
I'm going to scream!"

Pulled from the beautiful memories of my daydream,
and still struggling to process what I had just witnessed all
afternoon at Shibru's home, I stare back at my friend in
stunned disbelief, unsure how to respond her appallingly
callous comment. I simply cannot fathom that my friend
could so coldly characterize the intense suffering of the
starving and diseased, those lost souls who wander the
streets of Addis Ababa in desperation and pain, in a way
that depicts them as intrusive and annoying pests. It
seemed cruel beyond recourse.

And yet, haunted by my friend's words many months
later, I eventually had to admit that after enough time
spent living under these trying conditions, we've all been
there. The fact of the matter is that no one, no matter how
compassionate, is fully immune. We are all subject to this

subtle force that daily tugs us ever closer to indifference, in part, because it is absolutely inconceivable to truly imagine the realities of the lives of the people that are begging at your car, and vice versa. From the standpoint of those begging, you have access to luxuries they could never imagine. And by contrast, how can you truly attempt to understand a world where masses of people wash themselves in filthy water that gathers in a pothole in the middle of a traffic-congested intersection?

While the politically unconnected middle class of Ethiopia are relegated to a life that contains little hope of meaningful advancement (like those I had just spent the day with at Shibru's home), the poor of Ethiopia are trapped in a place where there is simply no recourse; stuck in state of squalor with no hope of making it to the other side of poor. Like Sisyphus of Greek mythology, their lives are marked by constant and painful exertion.

Here, there is no government welfare system to offer support to ease their burdens, and aside from a smattering of international charities and NGOs, there is no help. If you get sick, if you go hungry, if you are abused, you may die. The government does not care for its people in a meaningful way and the economy does not operate effectively enough to offer private sector alternatives. You suffer, you die. In between, you have ten children, and the ones that survive will eke out a meager existence and continue the vicious cycle of poverty.

It is against this backdrop that beggars are able to rent children by the day so as to appear more desperate to the passing diplomat or UN worker. As if the scenes of old women with crumpled backs that become deformed after years spent hauling heavy charcoal, near-naked men sleeping on muddy curbs with people and animals walking over their limp bodies, or the faces of dirty, barefoot children with gleaming smiles that don't reach their eyes as they plead for money at your car window are not enough to elicit sympathy and aid.

But in this environment, perhaps a rented baby may be just what is needed, that tipping point factor, to solicit a charitable donation from an otherwise dispassionate passerby. In a place where coping strategies among "the rich foreigners" harden their sympathies to the point where the miserable faces of the far-too-many poor slowly melt away into the background and become dismissible statistics, the crippled old woman may need the added compassion that a helpless baby generates to stave off hunger for a day.

I sometimes think that maybe the best defense against all this senseless suffering is to close my eyes and turn my back, to succumb to the sad truth that I am too exhausted to overcome a draining sense of overwhelming futility. Sustained compassion simply doesn't stand a chance under conditions where a hardening heart rots your soul in the name of self-preservation.

I try to explain this to my sister Jenny when she calls from her Norman Rockwell-esque home near Boston and asks me about life in Ethiopia. I do my best to explain how the multitudes of suffering humanity in time become forgotten souls that fade into the background of Addis Ababa's sprawling chaos. That they're somehow relegated to the shadows even as they tap on your car window, inches from your face, indicating with a quick hand gesture that they're hungry, yet communicating much more through their vacant eyes and shell-shocked expressions.

I try to explain how these faceless poor pick away at your sanity, to the point where you find yourself returning their pitiful pleas with an unfeeling stare before driving away. As I talk to Jenny over the phone about this world, seeking some solace from the guilt of creeping indifference, I can actually feel her face scrutinizing me with a look of sheer disgust, wondering how her happy, basketball-skipping little sister could possibly characterize the intense suffering of the starving and diseased, those lost souls who wander the streets in desperation and pain, in a way that depicts them as intrusive and annoying pests. It truly is cruel beyond recourse.

But as I slip ever closer toward indifference, there are times when, with that last remaining seed of human compassion struggling for survival against overwhelming odds, an occasional beggar somehow finds their way under my thickened skin to strike a personal chord. Not a faceless object outside my car window that elicits detached pity, but a fellow human being in need.

There is a man that I pass on my daily commute to work who has no hands. For the past month, I have seen him every morning, thin and begging in rags, on the corner of a busy intersection with his outstretched arms abruptly ending in stumps. One morning, while stopped in traffic at this corner, I roll down my window to give him a few Birr. The offering is the equivalent of about seventy cents, which he accepts with a delighted, heartfelt, genuine smile.

Lauren takes it all in from where she sits in the backseat and asks in a very concerned voice as I am rolling down the window, "but mommy, how can he take your money when he has no hands?"

At such a young age, my little girl is accustomed to the begging. She doesn't wonder why this man doesn't have hands; that is fairly unremarkable here. Nor does she ask why he is asking for money. People here are deformed and they beg. That is her reality. The burning question, however, is the practical concern of how this man will be able to take the money.

Lauren's innocent reaction is a poignant reminder of how far my family is from the orderly streets of McLean, Virginia where we own a townhouse. Our McLean neighborhood, a place that Lauren and Alexandra have yet to see, is perpetually brimming with fragrant flowers blooming in green medians, where bright, shiny, welcoming storefronts line the paved streets, and where traffic lights dictate order on the well-maintained roads void of wandering livestock and rabid stray dogs.

In contrast, here in Ethiopia, Lauren looks out her window and sees the sights of poverty. She no longer asks why a man is crawling along the gutter instead of walking on the sidewalk, his twisted legs folded under his crumpled body at a warped angle. Alexandra no longer wonders why a mommy holding her baby looks sad.

I haven't seen the man with no hands for the past two weeks. When Lauren asks me where he went one morning, I tell her he is having an operation to get hands, that he must have finally collected enough money. But sometimes, as I pass the now empty corner, I wonder what may have really happened to him.

CHAPTER 13

The Party – One O'Clock
Speaking of Health...

It's one o'clock. There's another knock at my gate, which surprises me – I thought that everyone had arrived. I look at the crowd again and realize that Mesfin isn't here yet. I go over to the gate, but instead of Mesfin, I open it to find Ira at the doorstep.

"Well, hello there. Couldn't stay away from the party, I see?" Ira works for me at the Embassy.

"Oh, sorry Kirsten. I forgot all about your party."

"Never mind, come on in and join the fun. Mesfin should be here soon too." Mesfin is one of the local employees that we work with in our office at the Embassy.

"No, no, on my way to the pool - kids are in the car," he points to his car parked just outside my house. "I just wanted to give you a heads up that you're going to have to give a speech on Monday morning at the Addis University on global health and environmental sustainability."

"Um, ok." My wheels start turning as I ask Ira, "So, health and environment. Do you know why? Any context regarding the conference to help me frame my remarks?"

Ira tells me that Addis University is hosting this health and the environment conference at its main hall and they want a U.S. Embassy official on their panel given the amount of money we give to Ethiopia to promote health care under the Global Health Initiative. The head of the U.S. Center for Disease Control (CDC) had accepted, but was called away to the field at the last minute to verify reports of a plague outbreak somewhere in Ethiopia's interior. The U.S. Agency for International Development (USAID) was the Ambassador's next logical choice, but this Monday conference coincided with USAID's annual staff retreat and no one from their health office would be in Addis Ababa.

"So, you were offered up as their last choice. Don't you feel honored?"

"Yep! Do you know what time?"

"Event starts at 10am."

"What about the audience?"

"According to the flyer, they're expecting about 200 - graduate students, medical professionals, health care representatives - a full spectrum."

"Any specific topic for me?"

"Nope, just that you need to speak for 20 minutes about health and environmental sustainability and then be available after the speeches and presentations for the discussion period." Ira hands me *two one-pager documents. The first is a fact sheet describing the U.S. Global Health Initiative (GHI) worldwide, with some notes Ira added in regarding Ethiopia's GHI "plus" status. The second one-page fact sheet explains the U.S. Water, Sanitation, and Health (WaSH) program worldwide. "These should help you with writing your speech."*

"Well, now I know what I'll be doing all day Sunday," I complain, raising up the two fact sheets that I'm now holding, but thankful to Ira for letting me know.

The situation makes me think back to a few months ago when I was attending an Africa regional conference on geothermal technology in Djibouti.

Three years ago, if you had asked me what geothermal energy was, I wouldn't have been able to say more than "isn't that steam from the ground - like Yellowstone's Old Faithful?" Now, I'm the Embassy's expert and diligently promoting this renewable energy's development, helping to position U.S. company investment and U.S. exports to Africa's nascent green energy sector.

Fast forward to this geothermal conference in Djibouti. An official who works at the African Union's energy department in

Ethiopia taps me on the shoulder. I turn my head and greet Yodit with a big smile. But Yodit is immediately down to business. She's a one-woman tornado, on a passionate mission to develop Ethiopia's vast geothermal resources.

"We need a co-facilitator for the next session. Can you do it?" she asks with purpose. No time for chit chat.

"What's the session?"

"Geo-chemistry analysis of hot springs."

Hmm. I got a C in chemistry in high school.

"Sure, why not. What do I need to do?"

"You'll co-chair with the President of the International Geothermal Association." An extremely prominent, well-regarded and well-known scientist in the field, by the way. "Together, you'll introduce the presenters by name and the title of their work, you'll thank them after their presentation is finished, and you'll facilitate the discussion period. But please, you must pay attention to the time."

Ok, so me and world renowned Dr. Geo Prez are to lead the geo-chemistry session with over a hundred in the audience. How bad could it be?

In fact, all went well. We kept the presenters on time, we interjected if they got off topic, and we kept things running. My visibility paid off in networking too, with me connecting several potential U.S. investors and a U.S. government agency to key African geothermal professionals.

Being a diplomat really is an amazing job given all the varied experiences you're exposed to and all the duties you carry out - developing entirely new skill sets and expertise, completely reinventing yourself against diverse backdrops in new countries every two to four years — all in the name of serving your country.

With this health speech now looming on my immediate horizon, and a day to get up to speed so that I can deliver a believable speech that I can also defend to a large room of experts, I can't help but think I should have been an actress. Diplomat had always been my dream career, even at a young age, but really, with all the A-list roles I've played in my fourteen years as a generalist in the U.S. government, I'm certain I could have won an Oscar. If only I were good looking!

Smiling on that thought, I thank Ira again for his diligence and say goodbye. Next I go inside to put my two papers in my office to keep them safe from the grubby little hands of curious little kids. Then, it's back out to rejoin the party. Duty calls - I have kids' candy dishes to refill.

CHAPTER 14

Opportunity Knocks –
Uncle Sam at the Door

I will prepare and someday my chance will come." – *Abraham Lincoln*

Growing up in the America's sterile suburbs, I was a daydreamer, my head in the clouds and my nose in a book. Fascinated by the world outside my window, my mind would often drift off to imagine faraway lands as I'd stare off into space with an odd half smile. Needless to say, I didn't quite fit in.

Trying to compensate for my awkward social skills, I would babysit three times a week, save all my money, and buy that perfect pair of size zero designer jeans that had to be zippered while lying flat on your back and pulling up on a clothes hanger hooked into the zipper loop. The perfect overpriced, undersized pants, but still I didn't fit in. I played sports, got good grades, joined after-school clubs, but gangly me remained awkward and quiet and just a little too strange.

Eventually my luck changed. Like many, once leaving high school for college, life began to appear brighter. Granted, I didn't make it easy on myself, choosing a college with a 7-1 girl to boy ratio. But I didn't have many options. While some may view college as an educational opportunity, to me, it was my ticket out. I had to go somewhere new and reinvent myself. Of course, the best place to reinvent yourself when you're young, blond, and thin is on the beach, so I focused on universities in South Florida. Mom and Dad Wivel, however, seeing high tuition rates and poor academic statistics, had other plans and insisted that I join the mass exodus of everyone leaving my high school for the University of Maryland.

After endless dramatic scenes and wild temper tantrums where I lamented the unfairness of my terrible life, my parents finally relented with a compromise. I could go anywhere that met three Wivel criteria: the tuition had to be comparable to in-state Maryland, the school's academic reputation had to be at least adequate, and the school could be no farther south than South Carolina. So, of course, I had to choose the College of Charleston, located in the southern tip of the South Carolina and on the ocean.

I loved my time in university and the four years flew by. And before I knew it, graduation day arrived. Don't be fooled. This day does not mark the end of tests and papers or the start of an adult, professional life. Graduation day is doomsday, signifying the end to a parent-financed life, the day my mom and dad officially stopped funding my existence – a forced financial independence, the boot from the nest. My problem was I had no wings and I was headed for a splat. My situation: I had majored in political science at a small, liberal arts college in the south and I couldn't find a job. In fact, I didn't even know how to find a job beyond something like lifeguarding or waitressing.

Desperately in need of guidance, I made an appointment with the college career counselor, eager to heed any tangible advice that this professional had to offer. I entered her office, explained my predicament, and she dispensed the following, profound bit of wisdom: "Don't worry. With such a broad major, you can't be confined or pigeon holed. You can do anything."

Like waitress, which I did.

ഇഇൢൟ

It was at this time, while trolling the university guidance center and career counseling office for job postings that I noticed an announcement for the U.S. Department of State Foreign Service exam. The test was free, so clearly the announcement was an auspicious omen for a broke and desperate recent college graduate. To be a diplomat was a career I secretly coveted, a job that lingered in my fantasy-world head the way some may daydream of reaching fame and fortune as a world-famous singer or actor.

But for me, having grown up outside of Washington, DC and my subsequent fascination with politics and international affairs, to be a diplomat epitomized the pinnacle of success. Telling people this, however, would often elicit a chuckle and a patronizing pat on the head, followed by the advice "That's very nice Kirsten - just make sure you have a backup plan."

So, staring at the announcement, poor, hopeless, with nothing to lose, I ignored the discouraging statistics on pass rates and the condescending remarks of the people around me, and I signed up to take the test.

I soon received test materials in the mail that included a description of the test, a practice test, and suggested materials to prepare for the test. It was daunting. The reading materials alone went on for pages and included titles like Henry Kissinger's one thousand plus paged History of Diplomacy. Questions on the sample test were as obscure as 'what is the capital of Burkina Faso?'

Reviewing the pages and pages of suggested study materials, I devised a stress-free strategy that would involve taking the test with minimal preparation and failing it miserably. I would then retake the test the following year, using the knowledge and experience gained from the first attempt. But on this second time around, I would embark upon a serious, targeted research and study campaign to pass the test.

According to step one of my plan, I ignored the volumes of suggested textbooks and I took the test.

It was grueling, but also somewhat encouraging. The entire exam seemed to be have written by someone who was interested in the same topics as me. Cautiously optimistic, I waited for the results of this U.S. State Department Foreign Service written exam. I knew that nothing was in my favor. With a statistical pass rate for the initial written test of approximately ten percent, my chances of passing were next to nil. But for some reason, I felt good. I had actually enjoyed taking the rigorous test and desperately wanted to be a part of that diplomatic community that knows the capital of Burkina Faso is Ouagadougou.

I came home from work one day, a long day of serving shrimp and beer to Yankee tourists, walked into my house, and saw a letter from the U.S. State Department nonchalantly laying right there on the kitchen counter in the same pile as grocery coupon books, applications for credit cards with only 20% APR, and an announcement that I may have won a million dollars in the Publishers Clearinghouse Sweepstakes. I stared, hesitated long enough to take a deep breath, and ran inside to rip open the envelope.

It said I passed. My eyes blurred. I read it again. Pass. It really said pass! How many people have the opportunity to see their most wild dreams realized and hold the evidence in their hands? I was elated and didn't know what to do with myself or how to react. I think it was a mild state of shock. But I recovered soon enough and got on the phone to announce my victory to the world.

It's worth noting that passing the Foreign Service written exam does not mean you're accepted in the diplomatic corps. Rather, it is your ticket to be invited to round two – The Orals. So, with pass ticket in hand, I traveled to Washington, DC riding high on my new found arrogance that came from passing the written exam on my first try. Forget the statistics - this was going to be easy.

As my confidence flowed, I entered site of the oral examination in Northern Virginia early in the morning as the sun was just coming up in the humid summer sky. And I left that building eight hours later a very broken person. I still have trouble looking at that building in Roslyn, the location of my demise. It was a full day interrogation and at each new turn, with each new assignment, I felt myself sinking deeper into the abyss of utter humiliation and failure. By the end, the pinchy faces of my interrogators actually managed to incorporate disgust and disdain into their expressions, with looks so transparent I know they wondered who made the mistake of allowing me to so wantonly waste their time.

I was that bad. I stumbled, I panicked, I wanted to cry. At one point during the if-then scenario with the examiners, my choices meant that I killed ten people. I looked longingly at the doors, envisioning putting an end to all of our misery by just running away. But the torture continued as I was plunged deeper and deeper into the back hole of failure. The dream of diplomacy, so recently in my grasp, was now far, far away.

Sufficiently humbled and demoralized, I returned to my home in Charleston. Having reached a dead end in my employment search, by default, I decided to enroll in graduate school. This time, however, because the tuition would be on my dime, I was no longer bound by the arbitrary Wivel rules and I chose a school on the west coast according to the newly devised Kirsten criteria: the school must be in a location where I could watch the sun set over the sea. I ended up in Monterey, California.

The Monterey Institute of International Studies had it all – it was on the west coast, on the ocean, beautiful scenery, and a good track record of government employment after graduation. Being poor, living in an expensive city, and borrowing massive amounts to cover the exorbitant tuition that I would one day be expected to repay with interest, I was acutely aware that I needed a plan. This time around, I absolutely could not graduate without a job.

I enrolled in classes based on their suitability for improving my chances of passing The Orals on a second go around, I took a job in the school's MBA department to have access to their business job announcements in addition to the seeing government jobs advertised under my discipline, and I applied for everything else under the California sun. In the end, I had interviews with the CIA, the Commerce Department, the Government Accounting Office, the Presidential Management Internship program, and many, many others. And, I retook the State Department's Foreign Service written exam.

On another random day, bounding in the door of my Monterey home after a long, sunny afternoon spent cooped up in classes, I was surprised, delighted, and anxious to find another U.S. State Department envelope lying on my kitchen counter. Taking in the moment of *de-ja-vue* along with another deep breath, I sprinted to the counter to tear open the letter.

Again, it said I passed the written exam! This time, it was relief that first surged through me, followed by elation and then disbelief. A second chance. And another trip to The Orals, I thought with mixed emotions of dread and anticipation.

After two years of signing up for classes that entailed delivering and defending thesis papers and engaging in debates, joining toastmasters, and taking on any opportunity I could find that would help me to improve my public speaking skills, I was ready. But this time, there was no arrogance. I was consumed with trepidation, but I was ready. I was going to beat those nasty Orals with their pinchy-faced examiners in a glorious day of vindication.

I went. I performed. And I conquered. By sheer force of will, I managed to beat the odds and I passed the dreaded test. This McDonald's-eating, CheeseWiz-loving, daydreaming, bookworm outcast from America's sterile suburbs was somehow finally on track to joining the diplomatic corps and I was ecstatic.

With my graduate degree in hand, and the two major test hurdles behind me, I was really on my way to being sent off into the world to be a U.S. diplomat – to facilitate the flow of communication between the United States government and foreign governments in order to build and foster relations to advance U.S. foreign policy objectives.

I was on the verge of traveling the world, living in foreign capitals and reporting to Washington, DC on the state of affairs within the host country where I would reside, looking at nuances in political postures and assessing how cultural norms are likely to affect political decisions. Nurturing contacts with renowned scientists and economists, meeting leaders who operate on the world stage, hosting events promoting the American image and our ideals and values, promoting American investment and exports, and explaining American policies and building goodwill – it truly was a dream come true.

I knew all this at the time, but had yet to learn, to really internalize, how lucky I really am.

CHAPTER 15

The Party – Two O'Clock

Vaginas Talk

It's two o'clock now and everyone but Mesfin and his wife have arrived at the party. I wonder where Mesfin is and am starting to get just a little worried. Just as I'm about to check my cell phone to see if there are any text messages, there's another knock at the door. This must be him. Shibru answers before I can get to the gate, but in walk Christine and Carla with arms full of food.

"Just in case you need reinforcements on the food."

Christine and Carla knew how stressed I had been about the food and the party in general, so they decided to stop by and check up on me. And, being two of the families in our dinner/ BBQ party group, they know very well that I can't cook. Their presence was a welcome surprise and the extra food was a big bonus.

"That's way too kind. Look at all this. Really, thanks so much. Can you stay?" I ask, taking the food platters from them to arrange on the table.

"Round two!" I yell out to everyone. "Dig in!"

Meanwhile, the three of us make our way to some seats that are off to the side of the yard in the corner and sit down.

"We can't stay long," Christine says. "We're actually on our way to Lisa's house to find out more about the Vagina Monologue arrests last night."

Lisa teaches at the International Community School that most of the America Embassy kids attend. She's teaches drama on the side and is active in the small expat theater community.

"Wait, back up. I didn't get any of that."

"You didn't hear?" Carla asks.

I shake my head no.

"The production of the Vagina Monologues that has been done once a year for the past three years was to take place last night. The people in the theater troop, mostly American friends of Lisa who had flown in from the States, were rehearsing before the show that evening when there was a loud knock on the theater door just before it was kicked open by the Federal Police."

Christine interjects to continue the story. "Apparently, the police were polite enough, but firm, and took the whole group into their police van and to a nearby jail where they all spent the night. The police said they were called upon to stop indecent propaganda."

"Wow. I guess in a place where women generally don't have much of a voice, it's no surprise that talking vaginas would be a crime."

Christine and Carla both laugh and then Carla continues "But hey, it's good to be American. Apparently, they all were released easily enough. Your American Embassy got them out."

"Lisa says they're shaken, but fine." Christine adds.

Carla and Christine were only partially right, but I didn't feel it was the time to launch into a U.S. consular affairs discussion. The reality is that these American women who were arrested were incarcerated according to Ethiopian law. Now, that law may not be transparent and it may be scandalously arbitrary from our perspective, but that doesn't matter. This is Ethiopia. This is their system, their laws, their process. The Ethiopian authorities can do what they want. Visiting American actresses, while in Ethiopia, are subject to Ethiopian law, however asinine and unpredictable.

That said, the Ethiopian authorities are obligated to call the American Embassy Consular section to report any arrests of American citizens so that we are aware of their situation, so we can inform family members and help to facilitate in-country legal counsel, and so we can verify that they are being treated fairly and humanely. We are not empowered to demand their release.

But, as the U.S. Embassy, the reality is that we do have access to certain pressure points. In this theater group's case, these points may have been pressed, with the police eventually backing down. The authorities probably made the arrest because they wanted to make a point, but not cause a full-blown diplomatic incident. So, yes, Christine is ultimately right, the talking vaginas were lucky.

"Hey, before we go, any chance I can borrow some sugar? I drove around to four stores yesterday and two today. Everyone's out." Christine makes the best chocolate gooey cake ever imaginable, so it's definitely in all of our interest to get her sugar.

"Sure, I horded bags the last time it was on the shelves. I can even give you a whole kilo," I offer.

"So you're the culprit — hording sugar so the rest of us go without." Carla says with a smile.

"Actually, it's not a shortage." Brian was on his way over to our little gathering to say hello when he stumbled into our conversation. "Meles (Ethiopia's Prime Minister) recently instituted price controls on basic food stuffs like sugar because he said inflation was out of control. Naturally, that means the shop keepers won't sell the sugar at the artificially low prices. What you need to do is befriend a shop owner and beg to get access to their stashed supply. And pay triple, of course."

"So is that also why no one is selling gas? I've been looking for days now and I'm almost on empty," Christine asks.

"Nope, that one is really because they don't have anything to sell. Ethiopia gets their gas from Sudan and Libya. Not the most reliable suppliers at the moment." And with that, Brian waves goodbye and walks off to make sure the guests are happy.

Carla and Christine say bye to Brian and tell me they need to get going.

"Ok. Tell Lisa to call me if she needs anything. And don't go through Meskel Square on your way home— the traffic lights have been out for two days. It's a mess."

Meskel is the city's major square. Used as a gathering spot for national rallies and mega religious holidays, it's also a place where several lanes of traffic converge into one nebulous blob that is impossible to navigate even with the help of a couple of the city's only traffic lights.

"We actually made that mistake coming here. In a city of five million, you'd think they could get at least a couple of functioning traffic lights." We all sigh on that note and get up out of our chairs. As I'm walking my friends back to the front gate, I hear an unfamiliar voice calling my name.

"Kirsten, Kirsten!" I turn from Christine and Carla to look towards the voice that is so intent on getting my attention. It's coming from a solid, stout middle-aged woman that I've never seen before. She makes a conspicuous beeline straight for me, all the while shouting out my name.

I lean in for the requisite three-cheek kiss greeting, but instead she grabs both my hands and bends forward in a solemn bow. At this point, all eyes at the party are on us and I'm starting to turn a few shades of red. Still at a loss on the mystery woman's identity, I'm about to apologize for not recognizing her when she blurts out in heavily accented English "thank you for my Mesfin. You saved my Mesfin."

This is my Ethiopian colleague's wife, and she is thanking me for having rescued her husband from prison.

CHAPTER 16

Mesfin – Jail, Circa 1984

"One death is a tragedy; one million is a statistic." – *Joseph Stalin*

"Local Police members came to Mesfin's home on Friday at 1645 hours and waited. When Mesfin came home with his children at 1700 hours, the police officers were waiting for him in front of his home. They approached

him and showed him a court arrest warrant. They took
him to a police station about 80 km from Addis Ababa. A
Traffic Accident Investigator told Mesfin that witnesses
claimed Mesfin had been involved in a fatal car accident,
and an eight year boy watching cattle nearby the main road
died due to this accident. According to Mesfin, he was not
in the place of the accident at that time and he was not
involved in any accident. He was in the south of Addis
Ababa in the opposite direction. The plate number that
was given by the witnesses is the same as Mesfin's vehicle
plate number, but Mesfin's vehicle color and type are
different from what the witnesses stated in the police
report. An investigation is underway and the local police
will come to a conclusion in due time. In the meantime,
Mesfin will remain in jail."

On the job, many are faced with unwanted surprises in
their Monday morning email inboxes that will set the tone
for their day, their month, or maybe even longer. Perhaps
an order was not sent on time. An important customer is
irate and threatening to withdraw an account. Or the
market took a significant downturn and large amounts of
money have been lost.

For me, I learn that the Ethiopian man who works for
me and has been working for the U.S. Embassy in Addis
Abba for over ten years - a soft spoken and dedicated man
who is universally respected at the U.S. Embassy - is in jail
80 km outside of Addis Ababa for a crime he did not

commit. And today is his third consecutive day of an undetermined term of imprisonment.

I immediately call our embassy security office for more information, although what I really need is some assurance. Exactly what, I'm not sure. Perhaps I'm harboring hopes that the Embassy has already sprung into action, bringing down the full weight of America's power to free a wrongly jailed, unfairly persecuted local employee. Instead, what I hear is far from heartening.

"Hello. This is Kirsten. I want to thank you for alerting me to Mesfin's terrible situation. Can you tell me what I can do to help? What can the Embassy do? When do you think he'll be released?" I try to sound calm.

The U.S. security officer responds with little more than a confirmation of the information that had been provided in the email: Mesfin had been arrested at his house when returning home after picking up his children from school. He was shown an arrest warrant with his name. He was taken to a police station in Addis Ababa for questioning, where he was informed that he had been implicated in a hit and run fatality involving a boy in a place 80 km outside of Addis Ababa.

Mesfin denied the charges, but was told he was under arrest pending further investigation. Mesfin requested to be taken to his home to change his clothes and, after much discussion, was permitted to do so before being transported to the remote jail closest to the site of the accident. He was told to bring his car with him to the jail.

"How exactly did Mesfin get entangled in this mess?" I need to make sense of the events.

"Kirsten, all I have is the police report. Looking at our translation, it says that a few school-aged children witnessed the accident and provided police with the perpetrator's license plate number. That license plate number apparently matches Mesfin's."

The Embassy security officer goes on to explain that after Mesfin's arrest and arrival at the provincial jail, the witness children were shown his car and they confirmed that it was the car involved in the accident, despite the fact that Mesfin's car's make, model, and color do not match the children's initial description recorded in the police transcript.

Mesfin later explained to me that when he pointed this out to the police, their reply was that there must have been a transcription error (meaning the license plate number is accurate but the kids' description of the color and car type was erroneously recorded). Mesfin also told the police that he has several witnesses that can attest to the fact that he was on the far opposite end of Addis Ababa from the site of the accident on the day the boy was killed and he pointed out that his car has no evidence of an impact, further corroborating his innocence.

Regardless of all this substantial amount of evidence in his favor, Mesfin has been languishing in jail for three consecutive days with no bail hearing on the horizon. I have to find a way to help and beg our embassy security officer for guidance and assistance.

"Of course we want to help Mesfin, but there's very little we can do. Mesfin may work here, but he's a citizen of Ethiopia and subject to Ethiopian laws and procedures. Also, don't forget that he was arrested for something that took place when the embassy was closed."

"Why does that matter?" My head is spinning, nothing is making any sense.

"If he had been engaged in a work-related activity at the time of the alleged accident, that could be a hook to allow us to officially intervene. Another angle - do you think there is any likelihood that his incarceration is the result of political persecution due to his affiliation with the U.S. Embassy? It's a harsh accusation, don't make it lightly, but if true, we may have some leverage to insert ourselves on his behalf."

Mesfin works on development issues for the U.S. Embassy in Addis Ababa. It would be a massive stretch to assert the government of Ethiopia is persecuting Mesfin for his work on climate change adaptation that would help Ethiopia.

"But he's been with us for over ten years and these are obviously falsified charges," I say to the security officer in what was becoming a growing sense of incredulous disbelief.

"Kirsten, you're not in America. Look, did you know that we had a group of Ethiopian staff here at the U.S. Embassy arrested about a year ago in association with a crime? They were never charged with any offense and their cell phones were confiscated at the time of their arrest so that they weren't even able to communicate with us or their families from jail. After two weeks in prison, one day they were just released. No acknowledgement of a mistake. No apology for the trauma. Never any charges, no court date. This is how things work here. And, by the way, in this system, eye witness testimony trumps all, even forensics or common sense evidence. It's guilty until proven innocent and it is incumbent upon the accused to prove their innocence. No Miranda rights, often no charges, no transparency. We all know it's backassward. But this is Mesfin's country, he'll get through it."

Ultimately, Mesfin had arbitrarily fallen afoul of his own system and the Embassy could not set a precedent of getting involved with local staff and their personal troubles.

"What about the conditions? Is he ok?" I ask, fearful of the reply.

"Look, he's in jail in rural Ethiopia. It ain't no country club, but it's not prison. Believe me, be thankful for that."

I hang up the phone and it immediately rings. It is Mesfin – the police had allowed him to keep and use his cell phone. "Are you ok? Are you home now?" my tone is pleading.

"No, no, I'm in a jail, do you know?"

"Yes, I just learned. When is your bail hearing? When can you leave?"

"I have no idea. I don't know what to do. I don't even know what is happening or why someone would do this to me, Kirsten. I didn't do this." His soft voice waivers as he speaks, despite valiant efforts to maintain his composure.

This is bad. According to the Embassy security, it seems like an obvious mistake and therefore and easy case for Mesfin to win, but this is the assessment of a rational mind operating within a transparent and just system. Mesfin's frightening reality is that anything goes in

Ethiopia because here, the individual is basically worthless. And his arrest charge carries a severe punishment.

In the immediate term, the U.S. security people explain to me that much will depend on Mesfin's bail hearing, but Mesfin tells me the jail is stalling the process of setting a date. And all the while, Mesfin is forced to remain at the jail.

Hanging up with Mesfin, I pick up the phone and call our Ambassador. I ask him for permission to visit Mesfin at the jail to bring him food and water (having learned from our U.S. Consular Section that these are not provided in Ethiopian jails). I tell the Ambassador that I need to determine that Mesfin is ok and being treated humanely, and that I have to ensure that his case is being administered fairly and justly per Ethiopian law. I explain that this is all I am permitted to do per our embassy security officials' guidance, and I assure him that I will do nothing more. The Ambassador gives me a green light and I arrange for a car and driver to take me to Mesfin.

Driving along the rural road on the way to the provincial jail in a large SUV, I speed past sights of unspeakable poverty where clusters of one-room tukul huts with straw roofs - void of electricity, running water, and toilets – dot the desolate, parched landscape. I am speeding through a region where rivers are dry and cattle share the few existing watering holes with people, the herders oblivious to the dangers of allowing the animals to defecate in the area also used for human drinking water and bathing.

Several of the tukuls I pass are emitting smoke from their grass roof tops, an indication that the women are cooking inside by burning wood. A major cause of deforestation, soil erosion, and land degradation, the wood burning inside the small hovels also creates a smoke-infested room that is a severe health hazard for the women and children forced to inhale the thick smoke over sustained periods.

All my speculations regarding the inhospitable and bleak lives of those we pass are confirmed by the expressions worn by the women walking along the roadside with their donkeys, with their heavy yellow jerry cans filled with water, or with back breaking bundles of fuel wood or charcoal flung over their bent frames. Their hard, firm expressions seem to lack all semblance of joy, faces that bespeak of a life of inescapable hardship driven by the endless toil to survive. These snapshot glances I am privy to as we speed along the country road give me the impression that these women might not have a word in their dialect for joy, that the sensation must be so foreign as to not even merit identification.

This "road trip" distraction, I am soon to learn, is but an omen of what is to come as I near my destination – the jail that is keeping Mesfin hostage.

When I finally arrive at the village where the jail is located, what I see is a gathering of huts and some corrugated roof dwellings that flank the roadside, nothing more. The jail itself is more like an animal pen; a small field of trodden grass that has turned mostly to dust and mud. The area designated for the prisoners is enclosed by a fence pieced together by wood, metal bits, sometimes rope - apparently whatever material that could be found to present a boundary area. Inside the enclosure, in the middle of the small field, is a one room mud walled structure with a thatched roof and straw-lined earthen floor. To the right just outside the jail boundary is the police station - this small building having a tin roof and concrete floor.

It is heart wrenching to see Mesfin trapped in this setting - a respected and accomplished scientist who has traveled around the world advancing U.S. development policy - imprisoned in the fetid squalor of a provincial crossroad outpost in the middle of nothing. Yet, ever-the-stoic, Mesfin holds his head high as he greets me, extending effusive appreciation for my visit. I give Mesfin a bundle of food and bottles of water and ask him for a full brief on what happened, his assessment of where things stand, and next steps to get him freed. That's when my real education begins.

"These people here, these police, they appointed me with a lawyer from this village. I cannot trust him. He is part of this. This cover up story," Mesfin's furtive eyes dart towards the police building. "He must be linked to the local officials who want to keep me here."

Taking this in, I give Mesfin the name and phone number of an Addis Ababa-based lawyer recommended to me by an embassy colleague that I had brought with me just in case.

"Maybe this is good, but I cannot talk to this man. If I call this lawyer on my cell phone, I must talk here, in this space, where all can hear me. If the police don't listen, the others (I looked over his shoulders to see the 4 or 5 other jailed people roaming around inside the fenced enclosure) would listen and report to the police whatever I say about my case and my plans. The police, of course, will use this information against me."

"But I'm told your case is good. You have the evidence you need and your first step should be to have a bail hearing so you can get a temporary release." Mesfin shakes his head in agreement as I speak, but his anxious expression implies otherwise. Not permitted to read or listen to music over the past three days of incarceration,

Mesfin's mind has been left to mull over his situation and circumstances. He has spent all this idle time agonizing over all the unknowns and the fears.

"You are right, Kirsten, but I am very frightened. You know, if they know my evidence I have that can prove my innocence, this could go missing. These witnesses who say the bad and wrong things, I am certain they will change their testimony to get the facts against me. These police - these village people who need to find a person who killed the boy because they are afraid - these police can rewrite my case and my arrest warrant. The original papers might disappear and new ones with information that matches the details of my car will appear. This way, they have better evidence against me. But maybe this is to say too much. More easy for them, these police could put evidence in my car. You know, it is parked right here in this compound. They made me bring it here. They have access. They can do things."

He seems relieved to have voiced these fears aloud, but his fidgeting, jerky mannerisms expose his internal anxiety. What Mesfin fears the most is that the longer he waits trapped in the jail with his car parked on the compound, the more vulnerable he will be to all these scenarios of corruption and cover up.

I ask Mesfin about his conditions and how he is holding up. He wants to avoid the subject, but lets a few details slip under a quivering lip. In terms of meals, nothing is provided, with Mesfin paying villagers to go into the little "town" and buy him food and water. He doesn't want his family to visit, to see him this way or to expose them to trouble. Mesfin tells me the other five or so jailed people urinate on the straw-strewn dirt floor of the dwelling where they sleep; a place that also happens to be infested with fleas and ticks. Off to the side of the sleeping shack, I notice there is some putrid water in an old, filthy rubber tire container that looks like people use for washing. Sheep and goats wander about, their eerie bleating calls adding a sinister quality to the scene.

To change the subject, Mesfin tells me he has forged a friendship with one of his jail mates. The fellow prisoner is a tall, elderly man with a weathered face and graying hair, his skeletal body stuffed into scant clothing about two sizes too small, yet somehow he comes off as almost dignified in countenance, stemming from a certain serenity of spirit. According to Mesfin, he has a basic education and serves as a spiritual advisor for his nearby village's collection of clustered huts, yet he hobbles with a bent back developed from a lifetime of strenuous labor. The crime that has landed him a two month sentence in the tin shack jail is having rented and cultivated land from a fraudulent owner.

"This priest, the gentle and quiet man you see sitting over there in the dirt near those sheep, paid money so that he could farm a small plot of land. During harvest time, an angry man walked to him and began yelling and pushing the priest. This angry man, the priest learned, was the real owner of the land he was farming. The priest said he paid money to another man. He did the work. The food for harvest is his."

"So who did he pay the money to?"

"Yes, that is the problem. He paid the money to a criminal. Someone who pretended to have the land, but he was not the owner."

"So why is the priest in jail? Why not the criminal?"

"Well, that is the problem. And my problem. The real owner, this angry man, made the priest leave his property and he also said the priest cannot keep the harvest. He said the priest tried to steal his land and he cannot do this. The land and the harvest is to be the owner's and not for the priest. But the priest said no. He wants to keep the food."

When the priest refused to relinquish his harvest, citing that he had rightly paid to rent the land and had done all the work, he was arrested and taken to court. The priest lost the case and, after wasting one month in jail during the process, he was then sentenced to a further two months in jail. In the meantime, his protest is moot because the owner has long since confiscated the priest's harvest.

The priests' main fault? Unlike Mesfin, he didn't have connections; there was no one on the outside to fight for him and protect him from the innate wrongs that had been inflicted upon him once he found himself entangled in Ethiopia's opaque system that favors the captors. The system had to punish someone, anyone, and the priest was their easy target. Case closed.

Finishing this story and back to business, Mesfin tells me that the next step for him is to have a bail hearing. Easier said than done. Three days after his arrest and he still has little news about what to expect.

"That village lawyer the police gave me came here this morning to see me. He gave me this bail request note." Mesfin digs into his coat pocket and pulls out a five-paged bail request document. It is handwritten on frayed and crumpled pieces of notebook paper.

"I can't even read what it says – it's written in Oromia language." Mesfin is from Addis Ababa and speaks Amharic. An outsider here in this village, of a different tribe and speaking a different language, he is an easy target for persecution. And, based on his well-groomed appearance and nice clothing, he must have deep pockets, an added bonus for the village officials.

Mesfin continues to try to explain procedures, despite his limited understanding, "I think this note must go to the district headquarters' prosecutor's office so they can consider my bail request."

The U.S. Embassy-employed Ethiopian driver who brought me here agrees with Mesfin. He says that while hit and run fatality cases are generally not granted bail, given the existing discrepancies in evidence, Mesfin harbors some chance of being released. His problem is that, as a prisoner, he is unable to deliver the crumpled hand-written note himself to the district court twenty kilometers away. Instead, he is at the mercy of the jail's police to do this on his behalf, and these people are not in a hurry to move. Mesfin and the driver agree that they are obviously stalling in order to extract payment from Mesfin.

Disgusted, I take the note from Mesfin, give it to the driver, and off we head to the district headquarters.

After driving past the place several times, we are finally directed to a small, dirt road that isn't much more than a walking path. Halfway down the rough, narrow road, we stop in front of a rusted, squeaky gate that opens into a dusty courtyard overflowing with villagers waving their multitudes of hand written notebook papers in the hot air at no one in particular.

The courtyard's periphery is lined with long, rectangular buildings that are painted a faded and sickly yellow and topped with corrugated tin roofs. There are no sitting areas provided in the courtyard or even any shade to block the now blaring afternoon African sun. And here I am, entering this scene dressed in my new Ralph Lauren tailored business suit and carrying my leather Longchamp briefcase.

As I walk into the crowded space with the Ethiopian driver by my side, we experience a parting of the seas as people make way for us to pass directly to the front of all the impossibly long and chaotic lines. The villagers stop what they were doing to stare at me in amazement, as if I am some kind of green alien walking in their midst, something long since heard about but not ever really believed.

Inside the compound, the district officials immediately take note of my presence and begin shuttling me from building to building, office to office. A curious object on display as I bypass the masses of downtrodden humanity that have spent hours or days waiting their turn standing in the dusty courtyard's endless lines under an unrelenting sun, the officials don't know what to make of me and seem to fear the repercussions of not handling me properly.

And yet, with all my sauntering around the place as though I own it, playing up my role to make a maximum impression on these local officials in the interest of freeing Mesfin, I never encounter the slightest protest. I actually think I would have preferred some objection to my obnoxious entitlement attitude over those endless stares of befuddled bewilderment.

In the end, after about three hours kicking up courtyard dust in the wake of my fast-paced shuffling two and fro in my Jimmy Choo heels, I accomplish the task of securing Mesfin a bail hearing the next day. The process required what could have been upwards of 100 separate stamps thumped onto that crumpled notebook paper, executed with a time honored, bureaucratic, communist hangover, officious flair. There were also a few handwritten notes scrawled in the corners of Mesfin's bail note pages by a handful of random, self-important, barely literate civil servants.

Without my help - the presence of a super power, green alien that can to jump to the front of lines in a single bound - there's no telling how long Mesfin would have waited in that jail or how much money would have been required to accumulate all those ridiculous stamps and chicken scrawls on his crumpled note.

ಬಿಬಿಂ೮ಿಂ೮

The following morning at the Embassy, I go first thing into the Ambassador's office with another request.

Recognizing the catalyzing impact of my appearance at the jail and courthouse the day before, which delivered a strong message to the police and local administrators that Mesfin's case was being scrutinized by outside influences, I want to be present for his bail hearing as well. I arrive at the village court by 10:00 in the morning, where I then proceed to spend another day waiting in that dusty courtyard filled with confused and curious onlookers.

I find a rock that can just barely suffice as a seat and begin to read some work-related materials. After about ten minutes, I stand up to stretch my already sore back and realize a circle of onlookers have loosely gathered around me to stare. Intensely self-conscious, I keep my nose deep inside my papers until eventually, about an hour later, the crowd finally bores of my statue-like entertainment and begins to disperse. It is then that I feel free to observe some of the drama around me, to witness the unfolding of base human emotion that, despite my inability to understand what they're saying, speaks a universal language.

A flimsy door to the rectangular building on my right suddenly bursts open. I look over to see men behind desks ranting at a frail, almost effete, elderly man as he sobs in helpless defeat. The old man is callously shoved out of the building's thin wooden door and into the crowded courtyard, the door coldly slamming against his back, rattling the building's flimsy walls on impact.

No one in the courtyard seems to notice, this mass of rural villagers all have their own demons to confront at some point in this place. The reverberating walls are the only audible protest to the old man's indignities suffered at the hands of these unfeeling provincial bureaucrats; people that have hurled the man from their room like he is a pile of garbage so they can carry on in their mundane tasks, sitting behind dilapidated tables in dimly lit rooms with cracked walls stamping hand written notes, their stone-faced expressions of indifference an unbearable sight in contrast to the elderly man's unbridled anguish. I have no idea what the man's story is, what indignities have been inflicted upon him, but the intensity of his emotion is vivid against the backdrop of cold indifference.

"Mesfin! You look well." My attention now shifts to two men greeting Mesfin in the courtyard. Having driven the two hours from Addis Ababa on this work day, they want to be present at Mesfin's bail hearing to provide moral support to their friend. We all gather around my rock seat and try to pass the time with small talk. It isn't long, however, until the conversation becomes more intense.

During the next couple of hours of conversation with these apolitical, educated, urbane professionals - now a huddled, well dressed group squatting in a scorched and crowded courtyard - they introduce me to a world driven by paranoia, vulnerability, insecurity, and fear. Mesfin's friends describe a life where one can be reduced to sub-human status on a whim, with Mesfin's story illustrating, they say, how a low-key, quiet, unassuming, non-confrontational, educated professional can one day, without warning, be plucked from a relatively comfortable life of Ethiopia's apolitical middle class to find himself sleeping indefinitely in a tick infested, urine-drenched hovel.

Mesfin's friends, now intent on making me - their captive audience - understand their plight, ply me with their stories. "It is simple. If you are not with them (the ruling Tigrayan tribe), then you are suspicious. Apolitical cannot exist in their paranoid and restless minds." They tell me that while political opposition leaders and other agitators are openly persecuted, low grade harassment of the ranks of those with "undeclared loyalties" is the norm. During times of stress, like in the lead up to national elections, tensions and anxiety are widespread and palpable. With Ethiopia's pending elections just around the corner, both friends agree that the general environment in Ethiopia - the operating space for the apolitical class - is rapidly deteriorating, with unpredictable consequences.

In this charged environment, even living a drab, sullen, inconspicuous, and laborious life with your head held low and your eyes focused on the ground is no guarantee against arrests made based on unfounded accusations where the accused are guilty until they can prove innocence. Whether a case of random, unfortunate entanglement like Mesfin, or something more targeted and sinister, the results are the same and Ethiopians are acutely aware of these ominous forces lurking in the shadows, able to pounce on a whim.

Listening to Mesfin's friends, I know that these stories are widespread the world over and not particularly shocking in the grand scheme. I know, in theory, the sad reality is that you could fill entire oceans with the tears of those who have suffered such wrongs. And I know that Mesfin's experience is unexceptional in this context, simply more fodder in an endless series of forgettable statistics.

For me, however, a typical white-bread suburban American, sitting in a dusty courtyard of a rural district court in the middle of nowhere in Africa, listening to these reflective, thoughtful, hardworking people open up to me to reveal their worries and their sad circumstances, this is real. Taking it all in with a heavy heart, I add a tear or two of my own to that universal pool of sorrows when Mesfin's friends dejectedly punctuate their stories with, "We are vulnerable. Here, there is no security for us. This is our way."

At the end of a long day, when Mesfin is finally granted his bail and told he is free to go, Mesfin, the driver, and I say our relieved and emotional goodbyes to Mesfin's friends. But as I walk off toward the Embassy car with Mesfin and the driver, one of Mesfin's friends comes back to me and grabs me by the arm, pulling me slightly aside and confiding in a hushed tone says, "Look around you. This is what it really means to live in Africa. This is our system. Our curse. It is not easy to be from here. I envy the freedoms of America. Do not forget us."

And with that, he turns to leave, his head held low in an attempt to hide the small glistening tear beginning to form in the corner of his eye, just one more anonymous drop in an oppressive world's bottomless pool of injustices.

CHAPTER 17

The Party – Three O'Clock
It's Easy, Stupid: Politics Bad,
Peace Good

It's three o'clock at the Bauman party house. The electricity suddenly shuts off and our ipod goes silent. The girls yell out "generator" and everyone starts counting, some in Amharic, some in English. This time we only get to three before the power comes back, but I have to walk over to the ipod to turn it back on.

"What does everyone want to hear?"

"Why not the radio?" Getahun shouts out. Getahun, our driver, is addicted to the radio from driving our car and he has improved his English quite a bit just listening to the English AFRO FM.

"Well, ok. AFRO FM it is. Let me go get a radio." I go inside and come back with an old, battery-powered clock radio. The DJ comes on with a half British, half Amharic accent. He's delivering the news. A very cursory update of events in North Africa. The crowd goes quiet to listen.

Once the program ends and the pop music returns with Michael Jackson telling us to look at the man in the mirror, I ask my guests what they think of what's happening all around us with the Arab Spring. At the U.S. Embassy, we have a TV in the cafeteria that is always on the news channel and the Ethiopian employees appear to be glued to the screen. But they don't talk. No one is discussing the events, only absorbing the news with intense poker faces.

During one afternoon when scenes of the Egyptians taking to the street were dominating the coverage, my husband walked up to an Ethiopian he knows and asked, "So, when does this happen in Ethiopia?"

The Ethiopian cast furtive glances at the others sitting with him at the table near the TV, gave a forced and nervous chuckle, and then immediately got up and walked away. It is just not a safe subject.

But perhaps in today's casual party setting at my home, having just spent around three to four hours together eating and laughing, people may be willing to open up a bit. Do they harbor hope that the Arab Spring enthusiasm could spill over into Ethiopia?

"Politics bad. Nothing good come from politics. Best is to keep quiet about these things and pay attention to important things for life. Like money to eat. Like good health in family," Fasika declares.

"But do you feel any sense of hope, any longing to achieve what the Egyptians are striving for? To have a voice? To own your destiny?"

"What do you mean a voice? A voice for what?" Getahun asks. "When people go to the streets, when they try to say no to the government, bad things happen. Very bad things." He was referring to the 2005 Federal elections in Ethiopia where many were killed during protests. Many disappeared. But at that time, the world wasn't watching.

"And now, we can fear some paranoia from the government. They will surely make things tighter for us now, just to be sure there is no, what did you say, 'spill over.' Kirsten, you won't see it, you won't feel it. But we know. It's real for us." Mesfin added. And yes, he does know.

"But what if this is a window of opportunity for Ethiopians. With the protests that ousted Egypt's Mubarak, to Gadafi's demise in Libya, and the protests in Yemen and Syria, maybe this is the time for Ethiopia? Maybe 2005 was too soon?"

"The time for what, Kirsten?" Tesfaye asks. "During the regime before this one, the Derg, they say that things were very bad. Very dangerous. You can't predict when they come, when they take you, or if you stay safe. There is no system for knowing about the dangers. Now, we know. We have a system and we know the lines. If you cross a line, then you are the threat, and this is very bad for you. If you lead the good, quiet life, you probably can stay safe. We can

195

develop and help our people to not be so poor without the danger of protest to the government."

"Do you agree Mesfin?" Brian asks.

"Yes and no. I do want change. I know, I have seen the other systems, and they are good for the people. They make successes. In my dreams, Ethiopia could be so much more. It should be so much more. If we could have a government where the leaders put Ethiopia first. To put the country and our needs before their need to keep power. But you have to understand Ethiopia and this whole region. Change brings chaos, and chaos is very, very dangerous. Look at Somalia. And Sudan. This is the wrong end of change. We don't even know what will happen in Egypt. I am anxious. I hope the best for Egypt and hope their country can take a good path. But think about Libya and Yemen. How many people will die in Libya, be tortured in Yemen? And for what? Maybe for nothing. It is all a risk. And losing risks for us is deadly."

"Politics bad, like I say before," Fasika adds.

"Kirsten, we have peace. And peace is life. We cannot disturb this, we must put up with the rest." Tesfaye says this while I look intently at everyone's expressions to try and read if this is what they all really believe. Sadly, I think yes.

CHAPTER 18

Dear Leader –

Behind the Corrugated-Tin Curtain

"If only Stalin knew!"

Ethiopia is the oldest independent country in Africa and one of the oldest in the world. It is also home to Lucy, the most complete remains of any adult human ancestor who walked on two feet. And because Lucy's 3.2 million year-old bones were discovered in Ethiopia in 1974, some to refer to Ethiopia as the cradle of humanity.

Ethiopia is also a country with vast, untapped potential. It is a land teeming with natural resources, with a diverse ecosystem spanning mountains, plains, forest, wetlands, and desert. In terms of biodiversity, according to the Ethiopian Wildlife and Conservation Authority, it is home to an estimated 7,000 species of higher plants, 277 species of terrestrial mammals, and over 900 species of birds. Add the tourism potential of Axum (known for the ruins of the Queen of Sheba's palace, rumored to house the Ark of the Covenant in the Church of St. Mary of Zion, and home to the mysterious obelisks made from single blocks of granite), Gondor (the city of castles), and Lallibella (with churches carved out of solid rock full of ancient carvings and paintings, it is considered by some to be the Eighth Wonder of the World) to the mix, and the tourist possibilities alone are enormous.

Ethiopia is also home to more than 77 different ethnic groups, most of which have their own distinct languages. A microcosm of this diversity is evident in the country's capital, where even an untrained foreign eye can easily spot the melding of culture and religion. A mere drive through the capital city will expose you to women sporting modern dress styles copied from fashionable magazines, complete with impeccably coiffed hair. You'll see the men in suits, pausing at muddy corners to have their shoes shined before they continue on their way. Also visible are women in headscarves, both the white cotton Ethiopia Orthodox style wrapped around the body and head in a pious, old world style, as well as the traditional Muslim head scarf expertly pinned to conceal any evidence of hair. Being home to the more strict variety of Islam, you'll also find women dressed head to toe in black abaya robes with only a small slit in the fabric for the two eyes to peer through and men with long beards, heads topped with the traditional Muslim skull caps.

But in spite of all these attributes, and despite all of Ethiopia's vast potential, current-day Ethiopia remains a poor and insular country, vulnerable to drought and historically subject to severe economic slumps. And in a country where an estimated 85% of the population is a subsistence farmer, chronic food insecurity and famine are pervasive.

ഇഇിരിരി

A Tumultuous History

Facts taken from U.S. Department of State Background Notes:
http://www.state.gov/r/pa/ei/bgn/2859.htm

This large, extremely diverse, and fiercely independent nation has been ruled by absolute monarchies for much of its secluded history. Following the 1630s expulsion of all foreign missionaries, a three-century period of isolation engulfed the land of ancient Abyssinia. Emperors Theodore II (1855-68), Johannes IV (1872-89), and Menelik II (1889-1913) all contributed to working to consolidate the kingdom of what is now called Ethiopia.

A series of royal successions led to the crowning of Haile Selassie in 1930. When Italian Fascist forces invaded and occupied Ethiopia in 1936, Selassie was forced into exile and went to England. But in 1941, after the British and Ethiopian forces defeated the Italians, Selassie was reinstated to the throne. He was deposed, however, on September 12, 1974 by a provisional administrative council of soldiers, called the Derg ("committee"). The Derg, upon taking over, executed 59 members of the Selassie royal family and ministers and generals of the emperor's government. And Emperor Haile Selassie was strangled by Derg forces on August 22, 1975.

According to historical accounts, the Derg's eventual collapse in the early 1990s was exacerbated by droughts, famine, and insurrections, particularly in Ethiopia's northern regions of Tigray and Eritrea. In 1989, the Tigrayan People's Liberation Front (TPLF) merged with other ethnically-based opposition movements to form the Ethiopian Peoples' Revolutionary Democratic Front (EPRDF). And in May 1991, after much civil war strife and turmoil, EPRDF forces advanced on Addis Ababa to overthrow the Derg.

In July 1991, the EPRDF, the Oromo Liberation Front (OLF), and others - with the Derg now deposed and its leader in exile - established the Transitional Government of Ethiopia (TGE). The TGE was comprised of an 87-member Council of Representatives and was guided by a national charter that served as a transitional constitution. TGE leader Meles Zenawi, and members of the TGE pledged to oversee the formation of a multi-party democracy.

The election of a 547-member constituent assembly was held in June 1994 and the assembly adopted the constitution of the Federal Democratic Republic of Ethiopia in December of the same year. The elections for Ethiopia's first popularly chosen national parliament and regional legislatures were held in May and June 1995. It seemed as if Ethiopia was headed toward a democratic future.

Today, however, after many years in power, the ruling Tigrean government led by Prime Minister Meles Zenawi is a firmly entrenched member of Africa's 20-year plus Prime Minister club and is coming under increased scrutiny from the international community regarding poor governance issues and alleged human rights abuses. Public election protests turned violent during Ethiopia's 2005 elections.

The U.S. Embassy in Ethiopia, per the U.S. State Department's Background Notes on Ethiopia (a public internet site), reported that in simultaneous national and regional parliamentary elections in May 2010, the ruling EPRDF received approximately 70 percent of total votes cast and won more than 99 percent of all legislative seats in the country. Election day was peaceful with an apparent 93 percent of registered voters having cast ballots, but independent observation and monitoring of the vote was notably limited. Only European Union and African Union observers were permitted official access to monitor the election, and they were restricted to the capital and barred from proximity to polling places. There was, however, ample evidence to suggest opposition candidates and their supporters were intimidated in order to influence the victory.

Overall, according to public State Department reports, the 2010 elections were not up to international standards because the environment was not conducive to free and fair elections. The EPRDF used the advantages of incumbency to restrict political space for opposition candidates and activists. At the local level, thousands of opposition activists complained of EPRDF-sponsored mistreatment ranging from harassment in submitting candidacy forms to beatings by local militia members – and complained further that there was no non-EPRDF dominated forum to which to present those complaints.

Regardless of these unofficial reports, in the aftermath of this highly questionable 2010 election cycle, the state-run Ethiopian telecom (ETC) spammed their population with the 1984-like Orwellian cell phone text: "Congratulations! Once again Ethiopians have successfully held a peaceful, democratic, and credible election! Proud to be Ethiopian!"

So, it is safe to say that Ethiopia did not experience a democratic form of government until the 1990s, and then it was only fleeting at best. From absolutist emperors intent on maintaining an iron grip on power, to the ruthless Stalinist-style Derg regime where bodies of political enemies were tossed into the streets, to the Tigrean political elite ruling class that systematically represses political dissent through intimidation and violence, Ethiopia has known a tumultuous history. Yet despite what appears on paper as significant change (from absolute monarchy to Stalinist-military-communism and dictatorship-democracy), these regime changes have been described to me by Ethiopians as little more than an exercise in changing the colors on a chalkboard – the actual writing on the wall remains constant. Because, through it all, Ethiopia's people continue to suffer.

Not so, however, for the foreigner living in Ethiopia's capital of Addis Ababa. Ethiopia's expat bubble is quite comfortable by contrast. We are not the targets of the regime's menacing grasp, nor are we the focus of Big

Brother's penetrating eyes. We don't see or feel the
oppressive presence of an ever-watching, ever-listening
Dear Leader. We are barely even aware of the pressures
and anxieties which the people of Ethiopia are subject to
on a daily basis.

Like a yacht cruising through the ocean, the rough seas
do little to upset the stable equilibrium of our strong and
steady ship. As our luxury, expatriate yacht smoothly
navigates rolling waves of shark-infested waters while its
passengers lounge on the sun deck in cushioned recliners
and complain of champagne that is not cold enough, we
are oblivious to the trials of the struggling humanity trying
to stay afloat in their barely seaworthy vessels that
crisscross our path. And so the Ethiopian citizens' secret
world undulates just under our expatriate noses without
our awareness, as we spend our time whining about the
noise our loud generators make when they kick-in to give
our homes instant power immediately after the city's
electricity is cut.

It is only in taking the time to talk to people and gain
their confidence that we can gather small tidbits about
their life, that we can learn about their struggles, to get a
sense of the real life that pulses on the other side of the
corrugated-tin curtain. From a conversation with my
Ethiopian tennis instructor to talking to a local employee
at the Sheraton, to a discussion with a student at Addis
Ababa University, the Ethiopian mother of my daughter's

preschool friend, Ethiopians that work for Non-government Organizations (NGOs), my household staff, and the Ethiopian shop owners that cater to foreigner interests and checkbooks – these peoples' telling stories, in time, paint a picture of a very different place, a different universe, from that in which the foreigners reside.

But why do the people of Ethiopia put up with this? They see and live with these two worlds, they know the contrasts of how the foreigners live. With the advent of unrest that swept North Africa in the Arab Spring, deposing entrenched leaders in Tunisia, Egypt, and Libya, will we see Ethiopians rising up to ride this wave?

Ethiopians rallied and mounted a plausible opposition in 2005, only to be rewarded with misery. Silence ensued and apathy now prevails. Yet despite this climate of fear and persecution, the majority of my informal discussions with local Ethiopians end with a seemingly honest and genuine assertion "but I like Meles. He is good for us." A universal belief espoused by supporters, opposition, allies, sworn enemies, and anyone in between, Ethiopia's Prime Minister Meles is widely regarded as a brilliant man and the international community has embraced his leadership on a myriad of international issues.

During the two-hour car ride to the rural jail outside of Addis Ababa where I was going to help Mesfin, I had the opportunity to delve deeper into this question of

Meles' leadership with my driver. After much discussion about the extent of repression and persecution, I ask the embassy driver, "Mesfin's troubles, could this also happen to you?"

"Of course," he replies without a moment's hesitation. But after a short, reflective pause, he adds, "but I like Meles." And he meant it. As do an astonishingly large number of Ethiopians.

How can this man, in the same breath that he openly admits his life is dominated by a centralized, repressive regime that lacks rudimentary respect for justice and liberty, casually add that he genuinely likes his country's 20-year plus despot? Was his afterthought remark about Meles an attempt at backtracking; a way to insert an insurance policy to cover himself in the event that his comments about the regime's draconian tactics had gone too far? I think the answer, most likely, is no.

This embassy driver's reality is that he lives in a country that is enormous in sheer size, he lives in a country composed of diverse and competing tribes and clans, and he lives in a country that is potentially explosive. His country is situated in the Horn of Africa - a historically dangerous, volatile region that includes failed states and nations mired in bloody civil wars. Like Somalia and Sudan, Ethiopia consists of a complex web of competing and often belligerent tribes, locked in perpetual conflict over scarce resources; a combustible situation that threatens spilling over into widespread chaos.

When faced with the options of living under a repressive regime (like Ethiopia) or living under collapsed anarchy (like Somalia), and if you believe there are no other realistic alternatives, then Meles' regime indeed becomes more palatable.

Journalist and author Robert Kaplan points out in his book *Surrender or Starve – Travels in Ethiopia, Sudan, and Eritrea* that for Sudan in the mid-1980s, "Democracy may have been wonderful in the abstract, but for a sprawling, illiterate country fractured by tribal division, it meant stagnation, chaos, and death…. what value can democracy possibly have in a culture where civic responsibility does not extend beyond the bounds of tribe and kinship?" And according to British economic journalist Martin Wolf when commenting on the 2011 events in Northern Africa, "the road from repression to stable democracy in poor countries with weak institutions and histories of repressions is long and hard."

Yet while the vast majority of Ethiopians I speak to informally seem to widely believe Meles is leading his country "in the good direction," I get mixed responses to my question on whether or not their lives have improved under Meles' two decades watch. The replies seem to rest on an Ethiopian's definition of "improve" and their capacity for harboring expectations.

A diplomat friend from the Netherlands Embassy told me she had served in Addis Ababa during the time of the Derg. This friend talked of a climate where government informants were everywhere. At diplomat receptions, during conference breakout sessions, or any place where two or more people may have the opportunity to gather in a public place, there were ears. She said that all were on a constant edge. Should she innocently say something to an Ethiopian that could even remotely be misconstrued in a way unpleasant to the Derg apparatus, that unfortunate Ethiopian person's body might turn up in a gutter the next day.

In the book *Man Without a Face* by author and head of the East German Stasi external police in the 1980s Markus Wolfe, this former Stasi terror consultant described his experience with Ethiopia during the Derg years. According to his book, Wolfe had been dispatched to Ethiopia as a terror consultant to advise Derg security personnel on the most effective and efficient methods to terrorize their population into submission. Yet in his book, when describing Ethiopia, he states, "the cruelest example [of using torture to extract confessions] was in Ethiopia, where the extent of murder and torture was so horrific that it was difficult to accept the reports we heard."

With the Derg regime setting a bar this low, the Meles government ranks far better on the repression spectrum. Under Meles, there apparently is space for expressing some criticism and minor political opposition, so long as you do not rise to the level of a "threat." The government does not throw murdered victims into the streets like under the Derg. People, generally speaking, know what they can say and what they can't. They know they are watched and they know where the dangerous red lines are drawn. If they go too far, they know the consequences and therefore can make informed decisions on risk taking.

An American colleague once told me the story she had heard about a well-known and well-respected Ethiopian activist who took issue with Meles' government policy on land leasing. While considering writing a letter of protest to the (government controlled) newspaper, he first consulted his family, his priest, his colleagues, and friends. After much deep thought and contemplation, he decided to stay true to his conscience and go forward with his official record of protest. But before sending off the letter, according to my friend, this man made arrangements with his family in the event that he should disappear. A calculated decision, while planning his strategy to peacefully protest a government-led land leasing decision, he also had to plan methodically with his family for his own demise.

Ethiopia's current system is now much less random. It may be stifling and lethal, but you know the risks and you know what actions can lead to your quiet disappearance. The bottom line is - cross Meles at your own peril. But who is this Meles?

An Ethiopian colleague told me during an informal conversation that he had attended the same boarding school as Meles and that he has older friends who had been Meles' classmates at the school. Fascinated to learn more about this man and possibly gain insight into this leader's character, I inundated my colleague with questions.

"You see, Kirsten, at this boarding school, we like sports. We play always. But there is only one basketball court. We divide the court in half, so there can be four teams playing, but still, there are more people than places. So, there is a system of winning. You win, you stay on the court. You lose, the next team comes on."

"Sounds fair enough."

"Yes, fair if you are honest. Of course, boys are boys, and there is much cheating to stay on the court."

"Oh. Ok, but what does this have to do with Meles?"

"Yes, Meles. My friend tells me Meles likes basketball very much. He is ok, but he does not like the losing part. He is a big, big cheater to stay on the court. He fights. If there are too many to fight, he leaves to get his friends and comes back to fight. Anything to stay. He cannot lose. Better to destroy the court than give it to another. You know what I am saying?"

"Yeah, I get it. He must win and won't play by the rules. It's all about the end, not the means. I'm curious, though, was he any good?"

"He is good at cheating. He is good at fighting. He is good at doing what he must to stay on top. He has one mind for this. That is what my friend tells me."

My colleague went on to tell me that one of his older friends who had been a classmate said that once, when riding a bus with Meles to the boarding school past a famous statue of the Ethiopian monarch Menlik II sitting on his bucking stallion in one of the city's main roundabouts, this student-aged Meles said under his breath "one day that man will come down off his horse," in a tone that sent chills down my colleague's friend's spine.

With the downfall of the Derg and Meles' TPLF marching on Addis Ababa to take the city, Meles' prophecy apparently came close to coming true as the rebel supporters marched on the statue. In the end, though, enough people in support of rescuing the statue to preserve Ethiopia's history came to its aid and the statue remains intact today. The people took to the street. To save their long dead king.

"Is Meles religious?" I ask. Religion plays such a major role in the lives of much of Ethiopia's people.

"To be honest, I think no. Not very religious. He has much blood on his hands from the rebel days, when he was rising in the ranks, and now to stay in power. I think in his family village, I have heard stories that the people do not even respect his family. I hear they say the father is not to be trusted – his character is bad."

"And at school? Did your friends say he was liked?"

"I guess not so much. He had the followers because he is a leader, but not in a good way. He is single minded for power. He does what is best for him. If it is best also for Ethiopia, then good. If no, he does what he needs to keep the power for himself. This is what I believe. Meles will never get off the court."

"But what happens next? Meles cannot live forever. What is Ethiopia post-Meles? Do people think about this? You say the people took to the streets to save the Menelik II statue, and Ethiopians bravely protested in the 2005 elections. Do Ethiopians think, especially after what has happened in Tunisia and Egypt and in other places as part of this Arab Spring, that maybe it is time for Meles to leave the court or at least that there needs to be some discussion and openness to ideas as to who will lead after Meles?"

"Kirsten, yes, the people once saved a long-dead king, but I must say we do not seem willing or able to do something to save our children's future. Sometimes, when I am very sad, I think to myself that people get the government they deserve."

And with that, he walked away, leaving me with the image of a corrugated-tin curtain closing behind him as he made his sad departure and left the court with a bent head and slumped shoulders.

That night back at home, I tentatively brought up this topic with Fasika, hoping she might be able to shed some more light on the Ethiopian mindset.

The night happens to be another one of the many evenings when the electricity has gone off and on innumerable times within a short period, and, Murphy's Law, it's also a night where my now extremely frustrated children are trying to watch a DVD movie. 'All they want to do is watch a movie, why is everything so hard,' I whine to myself just before turning to Fasika to vent.

"Fasika, why do you accept this? Why should it be ok for you to not have electricity? I don't understand why people don't demand more. Look at Egypt. What do you think when you see these people binding together to change their system, to make life better?"

Fasika looks at me for a few seconds, gathering her thoughts. "My father is angry man. He says things. Many things. I tell my father to close his mouth. 'Do you want to become in jail?' I say. 'What of your family? You have house. You have job. You have food. You life is fine,' I shout him. 'Why you make risk? What you want? You live good.' My daddy old now, he stops. I am happy. Politics no good."

"But what if that doesn't have to be true? What if politics could be good if you could have the right leaders? Leaders who listen to the people and make changes for the country, changes the people want?"

"Miss Kirsten, in Dubai, I read the news. I am angry. And why? For nothing. In 2005 with the elections, so many people die. Too many people. Better to look from politics, better to look at important things. My life is good. I am healthy. I am lucky. Everything is for God and I am happy."

I decide to go outside, Fasika's words echoing in my head. On a clear night, the sky outside my home is a brilliant canvas; the perfect backdrop to ponder the meaning of life. Or more specifically, the meaning of life in

Ethiopia. I need to reconcile all my conflicting emotions, intellectual confusion, to find reason in the absurdities, and to somehow make peace with the sadness of it all. But my musings are cut short as soon as I open my front door to walk into my home's fenced compound.

No! They're burning plastic again! This started a couple of nights ago and I was enraged the first night those toxic fumes wafted my way. I decide to talk to the embassy security night guard tonight see if he knows anything.

"Do you smell that?" I ask, holding my nose.

"Of course."

"You know that's the smell of burning plastic. It's very dangerous to breathe. Dangerous for your health."

"Of course I know. It happens many nights now."

"Really? I didn't know."

"Yes. Before, they start later. After people sleeping. Now, each night is more early."

"Who is doing this?"

"It is one of the homes," he points to the next door houses on either side and in the back. "Someone made a plastic bag factory in their house. They burn the plastic to make the bags. I no know the house, but must be one of these."

"But this can't happen. Really, the chemicals you breathe are toxic. They cause cancer. We have to do something to stop them. What do the others around here say?" This time it's me pointing to the neighborhood homes.

"They say nothing. They don't care or they don't know."

"But this is terrible. We must stop it. People can't be allowed to poison us like this. My kids can't breathe this every night. And you - you sit out here all night and breathe these chemicals."

"Yes, I know, but what can I do?" He shrugs his shoulders.

"Is it illegal? Can we go to the police?"

He laughs. "Ma'am, we are developing country. We do not care for our people."

But Meles is good. If only Meles knew.

CHAPTER 19

The Party – Four O'Clock
Seized with Fear in Thailand

It's now four o'clock. With the sun getting lower in the sky, the wind begins to feel a little chilly so Brian and Shibru get to work on building a small bonfire in the yard to keep the party going. As the loudspeakers of the nearby Ethiopian Orthodox church are just starting to gear up for their late afternoon worship session, our conversation turns from politics to religion to health. Shibru says he's feeling better. He says his leg is still stiff on his problem side, but overall he's ok. Mesfin mentions the wife of an Ethiopian U.S. Embassy employee who just yesterday died in child birth. He said that the baby is their third child, and the baby is fine, but the mother apparently bled to death from a routine cesarean section.

To break the tension caused by this sad news, I mention that I've had two C-sections and three cancers, for a grand total of ten major operations in seven years, 2000-2007. They look at me like I'm a ghost. How could a person possibly survive ten operations? I decide to turn the topic of conversation away from Ethiopia's hardships by telling them the story of my daughter's seizure.

ᏚᏚᏏᏏ

My family and I had been living in Greece. I had a two-year old girl and a six-month baby, my husband and I both worked full time, we could only barely afford a nanny to watch the kids during the hours we were at work, and no family or close friends to call upon for help - I was a wreck. With endless sleepless nights, eight-hour work days, evenings spent digging my way out from under piles of dirty dishes and laundry, and crazed weekends chasing toddlers and babies to make certain they didn't kill themselves or each other, it all left me a shadow of a person just trying to survive each passing moment. Meanwhile, the toddler bombs continued to explode in our small city apartment. I needed a vacation.

After much research, Brian and I agreed on a family resort in Thailand. We would spend a few days in Bangkok, taking the kids to temples and markets, soaking in the colorful scenes of a vibrant Asian city. We would then head off to the island of Phuket for a week of sun and relaxation. The beach resort had a kids club where we could drop off the girls from 9:00-12:00pm and spend a glorious morning at the spa having massages, facials, and other magical treatments. It was a vacation where dreams are made and family memories forged. Or so we thought.

The vacation began as planned, with an uneventful direct flight from Athens to Bangkok. We checked into the Banyan Tree hotel in Bangkok and I thought I had been dropped straight into heaven. It seemed as if an entire staff was there to support me and ease my mommy burdens. I felt the stress melting away. We dropped off our

218

bags, put the kids in strollers, and took a whirlwind tour of our immediate neighborhood, gorging ourselves on Thai food and planning the activities for the next few days. We adored Thailand, and it seemed the Thais could not get enough of our two little blond girls. I was happy again and it was a great feeling.

That night we went to sleep in the hotel with the expected amount of fuss considering the girls' bedtime routine had been entirely disrupted. Alexandra went to sleep quickly enough in her hotel crib, but Lauren, sharing the bed with her mommy and daddy, was far too excited to just nod off peacefully. So, we read many books, sang sleepy songs, told bedtime stories in hushed voices, and counted sheep, until eventually she succumbed to sleep on her own accord. Exhausted, Brian and I immediately followed.

At about 5am, my light-sleeping, vocal two-year old stood up in the middle of the bed screaming "I need the medicine, give me the medicine!"

Still exhausted, I tried to ignore her — she was prone to late night outbursts resulting from mysterious toddler nightmares. Brian stepped up, though, and tried to soothe her back to sleep when he realized that she was burning with fever. With no thermometer and no medicine, he called down to the hotel's front desk and asked for directions to a nearby 24-hour pharmacy. There was one just around the corner from the hotel, so off he went to get some children's fever medicine.

By the time Brian returned with pediatric fever medicine, Lauren had vomited and then fallen back to sleep. Brian, now fully awake and seeing that all was under control, left to go and have a peaceful early morning breakfast before the morning toddler madness would kick in again. I decided to let Lauren sleep, ready to give her medicine if she needed it upon waking. With that, I dozed back to sleep.

At some point, I noticed movement on the bed next to me. I looked over at Lauren and saw that her arms were shaking. She must have fever chills, I thought as I reached for her medicine. Turning toward her with the medicine in hand, I saw that her eyes had rolled to the back of her head. She had stopped shaking and was as stiff as a board. She was not breathing.

I screamed and picked her up. Thinking that she may have choked on vomit, I started giving her the Heimlich (only two weeks before I had taken a CPR class for children). Nothing happened - her entire body was stiff like a piece of wood and completely non-reactive. She must have been choking while she was shaking in the bed and because I didn't react quickly enough, it was too late. Still holding her, I ran out of the room, down the hallway, and toward the elevator. I pressed the down button, waiting an eternity for it to arrive, all the while shaking a vacant and stiff Lauren, demanding that she wake up.

A man came out of his hotel room near the elevator and asked if everything was ok. I must have been in semi shock, speaking in broken sentences as I said, "She's not breathing. I left my baby in the room. I don't know what to do." I realized that my face was covered in tears although I didn't know I had been crying, and the man later said that he came into the hallway because he had heard a woman screaming.

The elevator door opened and the man nudged me inside, taking Lauren and me to the lobby where I gave Lauren CPR while the man arranged emergency transportation to the nearest hospital. The hotel staff took the man up to my room so that he could bring baby Alexandra to me, while others went looking for Brian.

It was then that, with Lauren lying on the lobby floor and me hovering above and pleading with her to breathe, that Brian came walking down the hallway. Witnessing the scene from afar, he thought, "That poor woman, I hope her child is ok." Getting closer, he recognized us and broke into a sprint. Lauren had just started breathing again when I looked up to see Brian. Relieved, but still in shock, I told him to go get Alexandra — that she was alone in the hotel room. By this point, I had managed to entirely forget about my helper man altogether.

Brian left, running to get Alexandra, when hotel staff said my car to take me to the hospital had arrived. Off I ran to the taxi with Lauren now breathing but still vacant and listless in my arms. The hospital was just around the corner, a five minute drive. As my taxi pulled up to the emergency entrance, a pediatrician was waiting for us, taking Lauren from my arms and running with her into the emergency ward. The man arrived a few moments later with Alexandra in his arms. He had reached Alexandra before Brian, *and returning to the hotel lobby he found that I had already left for the hospital, so he hopped into a taxi and brought her to me. Meanwhile, a stunned Brian had gone up to our hotel room as instructed, to find an empty crib. He returned to the now empty lobby in a panic.*

The hotel staff, fully aware of and on top of the chaotic events as they unfolded, ushered Brian into a taxi and sent him off to the hospital where we were all finally united.

At the hospital, I was informed that Lauren had suffered febrile seizures, something not uncommon in children under five that experience a high, spiky fever. Although the child may appear to stop breathing, in fact they continue to breathe throughout the ordeal and therefore are not at risk of brain damage. The key, the doctor explained, is to keep fever down to avoid the seizures altogether. If they do occur, the doctor said that you just wait out the episode and then see a doctor as soon as possible afterward.

While traumatic to witness — evoking the unbearable emotions of a mother who thinks she is losing her child — I learned that these seizures are actually quite harmless. But at the height of my moment of panic, alone in that hotel hallway, waiting for that elevator with Lauren held tightly in my arms, in shock and operating on auto pilot, it didn't seem harmless and I know that would have done anything to save her.

It was a harrowing ordeal and I told the story to my party guests with my best story-telling flare. But the response by all was merely a routine shake of their heads, followed by a general recognition that "yes, these things happen."

"God was with Lauren," Tigist adds.

"Yes, that is true," they all agree as the sounds of a chanting Ethiopian Orthodox priest begins to fill the early evening air. "But did you really have ten operations?"

CHAPTER 20

Getahun – How Death Makes Us Live

"...the way that a society or subculture explains death will have a significant impact on the way its members view and experience life."
– Elisabeth Kübler-Ross

If you were in a life-death situation and could only save yourself and one other person, who would it be - your child, spouse, or mother?"

Simple. You would save your child. As a parent, the number one rule is to protect your children. It's instinctive. A child represents innocence and the future. With a lifetime ahead, it is the child that most deserves to be rescued. Or so someone from a Western culture believes. Pose the same question to an African, and the answer might surprise you.

I attended a cultural awareness class in Africa and was asked this question. The Americans predictably said they would save their child. In contrast, the Africans, short of one, said they would save their spouse. The rationale was that with your spouse, you can have more children. The one outlier who chose his mother explained that he could always find another wife and have more children, but he only has one mother.

Delving deeper into the responses, you learn that the African replies reflect a very practical approach to life and death. Coming from a place where average households have 7-10 children and some will not live to the age of five, this closeness to death inevitably serves to shape a country's central value system. It's not that children are expendable, but rather a fact of life that they die. The key is for those that survive to keep on living. There simply is less space for sentimentality.

An Ethiopian holiday, called Meskel, poignantly illustrates the Ethiopians' fatalistic character. Meskel is a deeply religious day that commemorates Queen (Saint) Helena's discovery of the True Cross in the fourth century. Taking place on September 27, the Meskel celebration begins with a procession, people dressed in traditional Ethiopian white garments, decorated with Meskel flowers (yellow flowers that proliferate throughout the countryside in late September), Orthodox crosses held high in their hands as they follow their priests toward their destination. Eventually the procession reaches a main square where the Meskel bonfire awaits. In Addis Ababa, the main celebration takes place in the country's central, largest square – Meskel Square.

The bonfire is lit, with people looking on in great anticipation. According to the Ethiopians, Meskel's lighting of the bonfire is based on the belief that Queen Helena had a revelation in a dream where she was told to make a bonfire so that the smoke would show her where the True Cross was buried. According to the legend, she ordered the people of Jerusalem to bring wood and create a huge pile. After adding frankincense to it, the bonfire was lit and the smoke rose in the sky and returned to the ground, exactly to the spot where the Cross had been buried.

But the celebration has another purpose as well, tied to how the bonfire burns. According to tradition, the direction of the final collapse of the bonfire wood will indicate the course of the next year's events. There are four options: north, south, east or west. And there are four outcomes: — famine, war, drought or peace. Many of the onlookers celebrating the Meskel holiday have known all four. All stand in the shadow of the glimmering rays of the undulating fire, hoping and praying for peace. Because peace is the only positive prophecy. There is no category for prosperity, for happiness, nothing to predict success. Only peace. But do the people celebrating this holiday, those rubbing charcoal from the remains of the Meskel bonfire to mark their foreheads with the shape of a cross, recognize that their peace option really means little more than not famine, not war, and not drought?

In this fatalistic corner of the world, mortality simply rises to the surface with a greater frequency and fervor than what we are accustomed to in the West, taking on a much more arbitrary tone. I continue to be astounded by the number of deaths that affect my workplace in Addis Ababa. Whether an employee or a direct or extended family member of an employee, there is at least one funeral announced every few months. The announcements garner attention and sympathy, but the responses in practice seem more resigned and fatalistic versus genuine expressions of shock from the loss.

Fasika told me one random night that one of our home's U.S. Embassy-assigned night guards had recently lost his daughter. I had no idea and was concerned for the poor man who must have been suffering. When I asked

Fasika what happened, she brushed her hand aside and said that she didn't know; the girl was older. That was the end of the conversation.

I mentioned this during a random conversation with my tennis instructor one Sunday afternoon. In response, he shared with me the story of the day when his son, a toddler not yet in preschool at the time, was at home with his nanny. On this particular day, the boy had a bad reaction to something – maybe to food, maybe he was choking, or maybe his condition was brought on by a fever – but the result was that he stopped breathing and went into some sort of seizure.

The boy's nanny, an illiterate and superstitious woman recently arrived from Ethiopia's countryside, let out a high-pitched wail and ran out of the house. A neighbor heard the commotion and came running. She stood over the boy and screamed. Someone passing by on the street heard the screams and came running inside the house. Seeing the boy writhing on the floor, this stranger hit him several times on the back, repeatedly demanding that the evil demons leave his body. The boy's seizure stopped and he resumed breathing, perhaps because of the jolts administered by the woman's blows to his back or perhaps the seizure, like Lauren's in Thailand, had merely run its course. My tennis instructor will never know. It was a one-time occurrence and his boy is now 15.

A mere two weeks after hearing these two stories, I find that I have my own story to tell.

ꙮꙮꙮꙮ

Death by Appendix

My cell phone unexpectedly rings on Monday morning. Never a good sign. I look at the number and see that it's my children's driver, Getahun.

"Good morning Getahun."

"Good morning Madame. Me sick today. Sorry, no work."

"Ok, well, I hope you feel better."

Great, now I have to take off work in the afternoon, spending one to two hours on the road to pick up my kids from preschool, drop them at home, and return to work. A huge inconvenience, but I can't complain too much since this is the first time in two years Getahun has not worked. To my knowledge, he's never been sick.

Monday night my cell phone rings again. Getahun says he still feels sick and cannot work on Tuesday. I can hear pain in his voice, and feel badly for my selfish reaction to his calls. This time I genuinely wish him well and ask if he needs anything. "No madame. Me fine."

I put down my phone and walk into the kitchen. "Fasika, do you know anything about Getahun?"

"He sick. Very sick for many days. The pain is in his stomach, I think he not stand straight. He says blood in the toilet too. Bad pain for Getahun."

"Blood? Fasika, has he been to a doctor, to a hospital?"

"No. It is for God."

I reach into my purse sitting nearby on the kitchen table and pull out a handful of Birr. "Fasika, please take a taxi and go to Getahun. Take him to the Korean hospital with this money. Make him see a doctor there. Please call me when you know something."

The Korean hospital is the best option in Addis Ababa and well beyond the price range for most Ethiopians. Fasika takes the money and leaves immediately, responding to my urgency.

Hours later Fasika finally calls. "Madame, Getahun needs operation. The doctor says something called ap-pen-dix. Very bad appendix for many days."

"When can he do the operation? The doctor must do it soon. If you wait too long, the appendix can burst and that's very dangerous. Please ask the doctor to do the operation as soon as possible. I will pay."

"Madame, the doctor says the same. Getahun's family say no. His granma, mommy, many aunts, and sisters. I tell them you will pay because I think you will, but they say no. They do not believe to cut open someone. Maybe the doctor cut and then ask more money to finish. Maybe he no know what to do after he cut and Getahun die in hospital. They are very scared for Getahun. They pray all day." I can hear the wailing in the background - a group of superstitious and suspicious women deciding Getahun's fate.

"Fasika, you have to convince them. The Korean hospital is the best place for this. It is the best for Getahun."

"They want take Getahun a place they know. Talk to doctor they trust. Is ok? I go too and then I help them to come back to here."

Unable to persuade the women to stay at the hospital, the group of wailing Ethiopian women draped in their pious white cotton shawls board a bus to visit their local "doctor" with an almost incapacitated Getahun in tow.

After the visit, Fasika called me to explain that the doctor examined Getahun and said Getahun needed a shot for his blood. Paying for the shot, the relieved family went home, satisfied with their decision that had saved Getahun. Fasika said she could not persuade them to return to the hospital.

But Getahun didn't get better.

The next day he was in agony. He called Fasika and Fasika called me. Fasika told me that Getahun was begging to go to the hospital in between howls of pain. I ask her to please go to him and help him again today. I said that I too am on my way.

Arriving at the hospital as fast as I could, Fasika tells me Getahun has already been led to the operating room. The hospital building is a rundown structure emitting a sour, putrid smell; there are patients confined to beds overflowing into the hallways; and the interior is framed by dimly lit rooms that do little to disguise the dingy, smudged walls. Looking at this, I reassure myself that this place represents the closest thing to modern medical care for Getahun and it is clearly a better option than the neighborhood medicine man.

After hours of waiting, the very competent doctor finally emerges to say Getahun is fine but that he made it into the surgery just in time. Getahun's appendix had been on the very verge of bursting. Had the organ burst, here in Ethiopia, the results would most likely have been fatal.

And that's the story of how Getahun came within inches of being another one of Ethiopia's many who mysteriously die untimely deaths without explanation. Reflecting on the ordeal Getahun had endured from what should have been a simple and routine case of appendicitis, I shudder at the thought that had I been born Ethiopian, I would have met my demise years ago, never to have fallen in love and married, never to have had my kids.

By age forty, I've survived three cancers and undergone a handful of cancer-related and non-cancer related operations. But because of the preeminent doctors and unparalleled hospital care available to me in the United States, I am a healthy, unremarkable, middle-aged mother of two.

Pulling into my driveway inside my home's compound at the end of yet another long and emotional day, I see the front door of my house thrown open, my kids running out to greet me while yelling with abandon "yeah – mommy's home!"

I stop in the driveway and start to get out of the car. Lauren immediately grabs my arm and starts pulling me inside the house, saying with purpose, "Mommy, lemme show ya sompthin'." Usually this is followed by "look, I can touch my nose" or "did you know I can jump really high?" But today, she pulls me into the living room and says, "Look, mommy, I can make music!" She grabs a random CD from the shelf, opens the CD player herself, puts in the disc, and presses play. The house instantly fills with upbeat music as Lauren and Alexandra dance around the room like little pixies.

The band happens to be REM. The song is "it's the end of the world as we know it."

These past two days were hard; two really bad days where, had many decision points gone another way, Getahun could now be dead. But sometimes life and all its 'what ifs' are just too heavy and you have to force yourself to let go, if just for a little while. To not think so much and simply be thankful for what you have.

As I look at my two happy little girls and succumb to REM's infectious rhythms, the days' worries, frustrations, and anger, and all of life's confusing unfairness and crushing complexities slowly melt away while I join my two little Sugar Plum Ferries in dance.

"It's the end of the world as we know it, and I feel fine."

For now.

CHAPTER 21

The Party – Five O'clock
The Man Who Saved the Children

A car honks outside my gate. I ignore it, thinking it must be at the neighbors, but Shibru, with his sensitive ears that pick up the slightest sounds, immediately heads over to open the door. Really, who could this be? I'm anxious to find out what this next surprise holds in store for me.

Shibru swings open the heavy metal gate and in drives Ted and his family. As Ted is stepping out of his huge Land Cruiser, he shouts in his booming voice, "I just heard you're leaving this weekend? Can it be?"

"Ted! I didn't know you were in Addis. Yes, we're out of here next Saturday. Just one week left."

"Well, I was at the pool with the fam when I ran into Ira. He told me you were having a farewell party, so we had to swing by and say our goodbyes. It's back to the countryside tomorrow, so we won't get to see you guys again."

Ted is from California. He has two kids and now two adopted Ethiopian kids – a toddler and a baby. Brian and I met him at the Sheraton pool one warm Saturday a few months back. We were all on baby pool duty, lazing in the lounge chairs, slightly bored and killing time.

"Your girls are adorable. Real beauts, those two."

"Thanks," I reply, grateful for the opportunity to have something to do to break the monotony.

"Yours too. Looks like you have your hands full!" I add, referring to the fact that this guy has two kids, a toddler, and a baby strapped into a Baby Bjorn carrier.

"Yeah, well. These two little miracles were a surprise to us. You just never know where God's path is going to take you, ya know?"

I see the look on Brian's face and know exactly what is going through his cynical mind…. 'Oh great, not another self-righteous, religious zealot, do-gooder.'

Ethiopia is filled with people from all over the planet, coming to this place to save the world. It's their mission and they often give off airs that they know they are better than everyone else around them because of the selfless sacrifices they make to help others. And these types seem to converge upon the Sheraton pool in droves. They and Brian are like oil and water.

Brian is firmly rooted in the Real Polilitik portion of life's philosophical spectrum. He's practical and a realist to the core. Ethiopia is a country of geopolitical importance in terms of the war on terror – it is influential with its neighbors and is strategically located within the volatile Horn of Africa. We need to maintain good relations with the Ethiopian government because we need their support when it comes to issues such as Somalia. And that's the bottom line to Brian.

Subscribing to this line of thinking, Brian just can't wrap his head around why the U.S. government spends approximately $900 million a year on average on food assistance programs in Ethiopia, with no discernible improvement to Ethiopia's food security posture and with no obvious advantages achieved in our political relationship. It is assumed and taken for granted that we will feed their people. So they don't have to, nor do they feel the need to be grateful. This is the U.S. job.

The Chinese, on the other hand, are cozying up to the motley of African dictators, building and/ or financing roads, hydro-electric dams, and other massive infrastructure projects that all the dictators crave. And unlike the nations that ascribe to the Bretton Woods norms and principles, the Chinese operate outside of moral boundaries – bypassing necessary environmental and social impact assessments, entering into deals with heinous regimes that brutalize their people so that the Chinese can extract Africa's natural recourses in exchange for controversial dams and roads. Business is business. It's a model that people like Ethiopia's Prime Minister Meles and Zimbabwe's Mugabe embrace with open arms. As such, Brian asserts, the

Chinese are rapidly gaining influence and sway in Africa, winning the international chess game while we continue to feed a bottomless pit of the never-ending hungry hordes.

"So what do you do here?" He looks at Brian, not me.

"We work at the U.S. Embassy," I answer on behalf of team Bauman.

"Cool." There's an awkward pause.

"What do you do?" I feel obligated to ask, even as Brian burns holes into my skull with his eyes. He obviously is looking for a way out of this conversation and doesn't need me to encourage the guy.

"Used to work in real estate in California, during the boom years. Man, I made a killing on all that fake money. Lived a high life. That is, until the crash."

Brian perks up with this turn in the conversation. Brian had lived in San Francisco for a few years after graduate school and the number one way to Brian's heart these days is to talk about the high life.

"Where in California?"

"Orange County. Yeah, life was good. But when my business fell apart — well, more like crashed on my head like a falling piano from a ten story building — I had to step back. To reflect, re-evaluate it all.

Man, I realized I wasn't happy. And maybe I never had been. More like empty. So, I went to this church with a friend that thought maybe some religion would help me to get my groove back. Little did I know on that day that soon enough I'd end up here with these two little munchkins."

"What do you mean?" Brian and I were both intrigued.

"Well, the church was showing a documentary about a group of villages in Ethiopia where the villagers throw babies and toddlers into the rivers to drown or get eaten by the crocodiles for things like their front teeth coming in before their bottom teeth. Wait, no, it's the other way around. Maybe, actually, I can't keep it straight. Doesn't matter anyway. Point is, the order of these kids' teeth determines their fate. Also, sex at an early age is encouraged, some might say forced. But if a baby born outside of marriage enters the picture, then more crocodile food."

"What the fuck?!" I elbow Brian and give him my 'watch the language' look.

"That documentary was powerful, man. Had me in tears like a blubbering buffoon. So, I talked long and hard with my wife, and here we are. The church made the arrangements for us, and now we're managing a rescue mission and an orphanage. That, and caring for two more kids. These two are brother and sister," he says, indicating the two adopted kids. "We rescued them, found that they were also deathly ill from malaria. My wife nursed them back to life with the help of a charity health care unit not too far away from our center.

239

The wifey promised to never stop caring for them, so we're now a family of four."

"Have you heard about this?" Brian looks to me.

"This? No. But Female Genital Mutilation is prevalent in many parts of Ethiopia. Also forced child marriage, which can lead to pregnancies in children too young and physically underdeveloped to deliver a baby, which can lead to fistula. (Fistula is a severe medical condition where a hole develops between the rectum and vagina or between the bladder and vagina after severe or failed childbirth). In the book Half the Sky *that I just finished reading, the authors describe scenarios where Ethiopian women suffering from fistula - crippled, involuntarily leaking excrement from the hole and emitting a foul stench - are left out at night, helpless at the edge of the village, for the hyenas to eat. These things all fall under the development catch phrase 'harmful traditional practices, or HTPs."*

"HTPs? There's an acronym for this crap?" Brain is indignant.

"Well, in addition to our orphanage where we rescue these babies and kids, we also run an education program to help change the villagers' mindsets. We're teaching them that what they do is murder. Not just according to the foreigner's laws, or international law, but according to Ethiopian law. But it's hard to get through."

"Man, how do you do it?"

"Hey, I ain't no saint. After a couple months out there, my family and I need to get out. To detox. So we escape to the blessed Addis Ababa Sheraton pool to cleanse ourselves."

"Are you happy?" I have to know. Has he found what he was missing?

"Happy? No. But I'm no longer empty. I have a real purpose now. And I'm making a real difference, one little life at a time."

This man made a deep impression on Brian and me, his story adding a new dimension to Ethiopia's endless enigmatic layers. It will be hard to say goodbye to him and his family today at our party, but we went through the motions and exchanged email addresses in my yard under the soft haze of a setting African sun. We promised to stay in touch, to one day meet up somewhere in America. To have beers in our back yard with no razor wire-topped walls, and reflect upon our experiences in Ethiopia, to hopefully find meaning in all that we've seen, in what we've heard, and in what we've experienced.

Or maybe we'd just put it all behind us, and only look forward. Maybe we could become people, like my sister Jenny, who talk about their kid's school play or the game-saving goal - not that last minute rescue of a little baby girl one minute away from ending up in a crocodile's stomach because of her top teeth had come in before the bottom. Or was it the other way around?

CHAPTER 22

Finding Meaning –
Individualism Keeps Us Free

"Perhaps hopelessness is the very soil that nourishes human hope; perhaps one could never find sense in life without first experiencing its absurdity." - Vaclav Havel

My sister Jenny has always been a strong voice questioning my sanity. Unlike me, she chose to live with my parents well after high school graduation, eventually moving out of their home to live with childhood friends in an apartment just a few blocks away from my parents. In time, though, life forced her to choose – move to the suburbs just outside of Boston, Massachusetts and live with her boyfriend, or stay in her childhood neighborhood and stagnate in her adequate, comfortably familiar life. She contemplated hard, but in the end chose the boy.

That doesn't mean she moved gracefully, however, with me picking up the phone on countless occasions to listen to the sad regrets of a very homesick daddy's girl. During one such melancholy call, with her going on and on about missing home, I eventually had to interrupt and ask, "What is it with you and Maryland?"

This is a place I left as soon as I graduated high school – my first opportunity to break the shackles that bound me and I never looked back; the memories of Rockville, Maryland's suburban wasteland relegated to the dim recesses of my mind.

"It's home," is her short and thoroughly unsatisfactory response.

"So make a new home," is my equally unsatisfactory reply.

"You can't just make a new home. You can't force it. It's a feeling. It's the place where you belong because of a history. People know you, inside and out, and you know them. You're enveloped in a protective embrace where everything is safe and known because you belong."

Hmm. I think she is describing my hell. It is this mortal fear of being confined or defined - boxed into a superimposed identity that is attached to you by others for eternity; to wake up one day and realize "this is it – this is who I am. This is my life and it's never going to change."

Jenny continues as I remain silent in my thoughts. "Here, in Massachusetts, I just exist. I feel invisible and unworthy. Everyone around me – Mark and his entire extended family – they all have an identity linked to their history, linked to this place. Me, I'm just taking up space."

She pauses on that note with a sad sigh, giving me the chance to interject. "Maybe this could be a great opportunity for you. Put a positive spin on this – you'll always have your home, mom and dad aren't going anywhere. But now you have the chance to build your life a second time, to create a second special home complete with all those elements you just described. Think about it. You never said you miss Rockville Pike, going to DC to see the White House, the shopping center down the street, or any other physical attribute of Maryland. You miss feelings, emotions, sensations. Those can be rebuilt. Just relax and give yourself time."

And she did. Within a few short years, Jenny established herself as Beautiful-Jenny-of-Suburban-Boston, in the identical vein of her suburban Washington, DC persona. She is the queen of her home. Never alone. Grounded and connected. Her place is firmly established and her future is known.

But just as Jenny was rediscovering home in Massachusetts, my own carefully crafted world structure was slowly disintegrating from within, as if I my life in Ethiopia was an extension of the Chinese proverb of "death by a thousand cuts." That is, until the day I was hit with a "gash-sized wound" - the shocking day I learned of the brutal murder of a fellow U.S. diplomat who lived in my Ethiopian neighborhood.

The tragic day began little different from any other morning at the U.S. Embassy in Addis Ababa. I was in a frenzy to meet yet another deadline at work when my husband called with a much needed diversion. Addis Ababa was in the middle of hosting the annual African Union Summit (Ethiopia's capital city is the home to the African Union headquarters) and Brian had been tasked with covering some of the meetings. While this entailed attending meetings as official note taker, some of his time was spent sitting around and waiting, with opportunities for unique people-watching moments.

Brian doesn't miss a thing and soon found himself wildly entertained by the motley crew of ruthless dictators led by Libya's wildly eccentric Gadafi. At one point, Brian was in such disbelief at what paraded before him that he couldn't help but call me.

"Hello?" I answer, relieved to have a short break from writing a cable, fearing that my eyes might get stuck in their squinted position after hours spent staring at my computer screen inside my dank, dimly lit office.

"I saw the femme bots!" he exclaims with glee, like a little boy who had spotted Mickey Mouse at Disney World.

"No way – they're actually real?" Femme bots is the term given to Gadafi's personal security team – apparently an entire squad of good looking, incredibly tough, women. Think la femme Nikita cloned into a full security detail. I can hear my husband salivating.

"No machine guns, though. Guess that visual is reserved for inside Libya."

I roll my eyes. "What else is going on?"

"Saw Mugabe walk by, the little shit. Tons of funny hats and far too many animal print robes. The place is a madhouse – each tin pot dictator trying to outdo the next with their massive entourages. But did I mention I saw the femme bots?"

"Yeah, yeah, you saw hot security women. Got it. Call when you have something more interesting to pass along, I'm done with the bots."

About thirty minutes pass and the phone rings again. Brian.

"You really are bored. Any shoot outs? More famous faces? An internal femme bot rivalry complete with hair pulling and a topless pillow fight?"

"You haven't heard the news?" He is deadpan serious and completely out of character.

"No. What news?"

"Tom is dead. His body was found in his house this morning by Embassy security guards."

Ethiopia was Tom's first assignment in the Foreign Service. He was young, single, bright, and personable. He also lived two houses down from my family, on the same street.

"What happened?"

"I don't know. The Embassy is calling a town hall meeting for American employees today in an hour. I'll be there. My hunch is that it was a suicide, but we'll see."

I didn't know Tom well, but he had arrived in country the same month that we did. Because it takes a few months for your car to arrive by boat, the newbies carpool to work together in an Embassy shuttle van. So for the first few months, I was afforded the opportunity to idly chat with this young guy on our forty minute commute to and from work. He was sweet, gentle, and seemed genuinely kind. His abrupt loss is a shock.

It is in this saddened, somewhat confused state, that I arrived at the town hall meeting to learn the details of Tom's death. The faces in the room were stunned as we awaited more news.

Tom's death was confirmed, but we were told it was not self-inflicted. Because of the ongoing investigation, however, as well as U.S. privacy laws, the Embassy was unable to provide us with any additional details. They said they ultimately just don't know very much at this point, whether it was a random act of opportunity, something targeted, or an act of terrorism.

I go numb. This is not the news I had expected. My children are two houses down from Tom's. I need to get to them.

Somebody asks if there are to be any changes to our security posture? Answer – not at this time. Do they expect or anticipate further acts? Answer – too soon to say. Were there any tips in intelligence reporting that could have averted the death? Anything to indicate future trends? Answer – that type of information cannot be disclosed.

The meeting ended with far too many unanswered questions. While I was saddened by the tragic loss of a murdered colleague, my instincts as a mother - a mother in a tough and unfamiliar part of the world, approximately forty minutes away from her young daughters that are only two houses down from the scene of a potential deadly terrorist attack – left me gripped by the dire need to get home to them immediately. Brian and I went straight to our car and sped home as fast as our SUV would take us so that we could embrace our children in a giant, protective hug.

The girls were fine when we arrived at the house, painting quietly in their playroom. The neighborhood was calm, quiet, and unexceptional. The atmosphere was eerily unchanged despite what had occurred right in our midst as we had slept through the previous night.

I called my family in America to warn them of the incident and provide reassuring details before the news might possibly hit the international press and perhaps reach them. While my parents were sufficiently placated by my description of the events, Jenny wasn't fooled by my sugar-coated rendition of the murder. Instead, she pleaded with me to come home, asking a basic, fundamental question "what are you doing over there?"

"I'm serving my country, doing what I signed up to do," was my immediate, almost knee-jerk response.

Over the next few days, more and more information is leaked regarding the details of Tom's death. It turned out to be a result of a personal connection and therefore not of particular relevance to the security stature of the American Embassy community as a whole. The murder was not an act of violence against America or an indication of a surge in violent crime in our neighborhood.

As our embassy continued to sadly mourn the loss of this promising young man, life eventually moved on and resumed its old patterns. But I can't dismiss or forget the fear I felt, the feelings of intense vulnerability you experience when confronted with danger far from home. Convinced that my children were in harm's way, I had no way to reach them quickly, no one to call for help.

In the post 9-11 world, it is all too apparent that no one is safe from the far reaching tentacles of terrorism. According to State Department security advisories, evidence indicates that "the overseas security environment generally remains hazardous, with many extremist groups and individuals intent on promoting political and ideological causes through violence and social disruptions. In many instances, American and U.S. interests appear to be targeted intentionally. There is need for constant vigilance and awareness of surroundings to avoid of potentially dangerous situations."

I was serving in Paris during the attacks on the United States. Being overseas, I was not able to bond with my fellow countrymen when Americans at home pulled together as a nation, collectively recovering from shock and trying to overcome sorrow. I was relegated to witnessing this phenomenon from afar, via television broadcasts and amid streaming tears.

Watching both the grand heroic acts and those small, selfless gestures of kindness extended from American to American, I yearned to return home to be with my parents and sisters. But as far away from home and family as I was during this time of great crisis, I was profoundly touched by the genuine and spontaneous outpouring of support that came from the French people as they descended upon the U.S. Embassy in Paris in droves to deposit flowers of sympathy and support on our embassy's threshold, a symbolic act of solidarity with America as we mourned.

Even while Brian and I were serving in Greece, now as a married couple with kids on the way, the U.S. Embassy was attacked by a rocket-propelled grenade. It was launched early in the morning hours by an anti-American group when only a few embassy staff were in the building.

The rocket ended up going through the embassy's front window on the top floor and landing in a bathroom, causing minimal structural damage and no injuries. In this case, although the attack was a disconcerting reminder of the risks associated with our lifestyle, in reality, the incident ended up being little more than a nuisance.

Tom's death in Ethiopia was not an anti-American attack; it was not an act of terrorism. But it was a murder of a U.S. diplomat that took place in the Horn of Africa – a tough, violent, and dangerous neighborhood – and it took place where my family lives, two houses down from where my children merrily play on their swing sets, giggling about touching the sky with their feet as they endlessly swing back and forth.

This murder took place in a country where government officials extort money from small shop keepers and burn down properties where they wish to acquire land. It took place where illiterate and jobless members of the ruling tribe are given grand homes in the capital city; a gift received because of their tribal affinity, and an act of bribery to ensure political loyalty. It happened where people can be arbitrarily plucked from their homes and placed in jail, gone for a week, a month, six months, forever. It happened in a country where the economy is on the verge of collapse with no safety net in place; in a place where countless numbers face chronic famine, where too many die needless and untimely deaths, and where children are taken from their mothers in an act of survival.

It happened in a world distracted and beset by its own weighty problems, where little attention is given to the life and death struggles of the people of Ethiopia. It happened two houses down from my home where my children play and it sent my world spinning.

This jarring shock to my rapidly disintegrating expatriate bubble left me anxious, and fiercely protective. I instructed Shibru that under no circumstances was he ever to open our front gate to a stranger, never to let anyone onto our compound who wasn't personally cleared in advance by Brian or me, and insisted that the Fasika and Tigist were never to take the children out of our home's walled compound – that unless in our car en route to somewhere pre-cleared, the children were to remain safely inside our fortress compound, behind the locked gate and under the protection of our thick razor wire walls.

But despite these perhaps draconian precautions, doubt continues to linger as even my high, imposing, protective security walls cast dark shadows of uncertainty into what had once been my reasonably safe world on the side of the fence where the grass is greener.

It is against this tenuous backdrop, a time when I felt everything I knew was crumbling around me, that my parents called me to tell me doggie Wendyll's time had come. Unable to make the trip to Ethiopia, Wendyll had retired to my parents' rural home on the Chesapeake Bay to live out the rest of his days in comfort and peace. But now, according to my parents, Wendyll was losing his battle with cancer. Having put up a valiant fight, my parents reluctantly came to the conclusion that it was cruel to allow him to continue in his state.

While still lucid and very much the beloved Wendyll, the cancer in his mouth could no longer endure operations and it was spreading. Eating was nearly impossible, bleeding at times was profuse, and the pain was unbearable despite pain medications. On the day and time of Wendyll's passing, I was crippled with sadness thousands of miles away in Africa. Wendyll had been living with my parents for several years now, and was very disconnected from my current life as a mommy of two toddlers in Ethiopia, but the sense of loss I experienced from his distant passing was piercing.

Such is another luxury that I have learned to appreciate during my time in Africa. I had the great fortune to spend my free-spirited 20s with an amazing dog at my side. While I never took Wendyll for granted, I most certainly never questioned my right to have, love, and provide for my four-legged companion.

In a land where the description of the loss of a daughter is delivered with a dismissive hand gesture, and where horribly deformed beggars plead for meager handouts so they can continue to eke out an existence under unspeakable conditions, Wendyll's passing affected me to my core, but guilt compelled me to keep my sorrow to myself and I grieved silently. It wasn't until a trip back to the U.S., where I visited my parents and we buried Wendyll in a small ceremony full of emotional outpouring, that I was able to get the closure I needed.

In my small speech at the site of Wendyll's resting place, I told him that I missed him. I missed the way he greeted me with genuine joy every day when I'd come home from work; I missed our daily morning walks where together we would greet the day, no matter how cold or dreary; I missed all of our adventures, venturing out to explore new places all over the world with him at my side; I missed his calming, quiet demeanor that soothed me in even the most stressful times; I missed watching him run – a picture of exhilaration, taking joy in simple pleasures; I missed his big, brown, expressive eyes that truly communicated his feelings and unconditional love; and mostly I missed his companionship – he was my best buddy, at my side at every stage as I forged my path in life, and he became a part of me in that journey. I told him that he was always so much more than a pet or a friend and his gentle spirit will forever live on in my heart.

And then I cried.

In Africa, many children die before age five and spouses are not necessarily chosen after much soul searching to determine whether the person is "the one." With this in mind, I can't help but think how strange this burial scene of my cherished dog would have seemed to the African who might overlook saving their child in lieu of another family member because, in the harsh world that they inhabit, their children are replaceable. They have to be.

Staring off at my African home's fortress wall that separates worlds, I find myself increasingly longing for a place where security fences are not needed to keep the world at bay, to live in a place where children don't needlessly die in vast numbers, where people are not unjustly carted off to prison, and where the sick and handicapped have a reasonable expectation to survive and live with some semblance of dignity. I long to live in a place where it is acceptable to openly grieve the loss of an adored pet.

It is during these moments that I think of Tom's mother - proud of her diplomat son serving his country in far off Ethiopia - picking up the phone one day to be told he is gone. And it is on this sad note that I am left with the nagging question that my perceptive sister recently voiced – why am I here? My answer has to be more than a memorized, professional response. I have to find a deeper, more personal meaning to this three-year, emotional journey in Africa.

Perhaps the hardest adjustment for me in Ethiopia has been experiencing, and coming to terms with, the defeat of optimism. That, in Africa, life often feels like an exercise of bailing with a thimble, that all who occupy the continent of Africa under the impression that change is possible, are really doing little more than spending their lives throwing stones into the ocean.

Staring at the vast cultural divide which envelops me, my disenchantment with Africa rapidly gaining ground as I witness a world of cruelty, am co-opted into a world of indifference, and am raising my kids in an insecure environment that quivers under the omnipresent threat of storm clouds, I ponder the forces that create and sustain my two worlds.

And as I dig deep for answers to questions I had never even thought to pose before living in Ethiopia, my worldview shattered and a withering of faith in humanity taking hold, I find myself drawn to the notion of human dignity and one of Mark Twain's quotes: "We [the United

States] are called the nation of inventors. And we are. We could still claim that title and wear its loftiest honors if we had stopped with the first thing we ever invented, which was human liberty."

In Ethiopia, the concepts of human dignity, human liberty, individual human worth, and inherent human value appear grossly underdeveloped, enabling its own citizens to largely disregard or dismiss the pervasive and intense suffering of their fellow Ethiopians.

Perhaps internalizing the concepts of human dignity and the inherent worth and value of the individual as a fellow person represents the first step toward developing a civilized society that can and will confront society's ills. Until people view their fellow human in need as something more than an unworthy member of another tribe, or someone who is fatalistically suffering their pre-ordained lot in life and therefore of no concern to others, or someone whose plight represents an example that you need to get what you can while you can because you never know when the political winds may shift and you find yourself looking at the opposite end of a rebel's gun, it is difficult to envision meaningful change.

Nurturing respect for the inherent value of the individual human the world over must be fundamental to development and progress. It is a stepping stone toward developing fair and just societies, toward promoting the evolution of democracy. Toward creating stability, building wealth, and instilling hope. Toward cementing freedom.

Because, simply stated, it is our individualism that keeps us free.

CHAPTER 23

The Party – The Evening Goodbyes
Bland is the New Grey

It's after six o'clock and the equator sun is nearing the end of its descent. The bouncy castle man unplugs his castle and begins packing up as it deflates with a tired sigh. All the kids are yawning from their very busy day, now inside watching movies and eating popcorn, surrounded by mounds of toys.

As our conversation slowly winds down in the dusk hours, with all of us gathered around our outdoor bonfire as we finish the last of the food, I turn my house staff's attention to our last pile of give aways.

"Please, take these."

They all say thank you, with Fasika and Tigist and I tearing up a little at the finality of the moment. This really is the end and Brian, the girls, and I are actually leaving. Next weekend.

"No, no, this is my thanks to you. Today is my day to honor you, each of you. To your hopes and dreams, for you and your kids," I say looking at Tigist and Shibru. "For all that you are," I look at Fasika. "For all that you do," I look at Mesfin and Tesfaye. "And all that you will do." I look at Getahun. "Thank you for everything, for making our stay here the best it could be, for bringing Ethiopia alive."

As I delivered this impromptu speech, it hit me how much I meant it. Yes, I am thrilled to be leaving Ethiopia, to be putting this challenging place behind me to return to the blessed familiar, where life is easy, life is good, and life is blissfully and predictably bland. In fact, I'm ecstatic at the thought of soon being free of Ethiopia's demoralizing and relentless crushing shades of grey; relieved to give my conscience a reprieve from the guilt and a constant search for meaning.

Yet, in bringing Ethiopia alive for me, in exposing me to the many facets of their world, these special people have unknowingly helped me to find my way home. And for that, I am very grateful.

Brian suddenly pipes in to break the uncomfortable silence that had consumed us all, "Hey, does this mean the party's over?"

Tesfaye protests "no way, let's dance!" And everyone jumps up to dance in the glow of the setting sun. As for me, well, I successfully avoid the dance floor by running to the house to turn up the music.

CHAPTER 24

America – There's No Place Like Home

"A man travels the world in search of what he needs, and returns home to find it." – George Moore, Irish novelist

Why does Africa continue to lag behind the rest of the world? More specific to my circumstances, why is Ethiopia still so poor? This is the question that people back home continuously ask me, seeking my insights from my vantage point on the ground. It is a question that I grappled with when I first arrived as I tried to come to terms with the complexities of Africa. It is a question that continues to haunt scholars and experts after many decades of research and analysis.

Is it the lack of education which creates a systematic lack of capacity and technical expertise to run the continent's individual countries even at a basic level? Is it the poor health conditions that render vast segments of its population sick and lethargic? Generations suffering from malnutrition, the prevalence of untreated disease and parasites? Is it a lack of access to basic human needs such as clean water and electricity? Is it a defunct economy, rampant corruption, or the brain drain phenomenon? Is it colonial legacies, tribal rivalry, or the enduring effects of conflict and war? Or perhaps it is an underdeveloped concept of inherent human worth and value?

The key to addressing these questions must lie in the acceptance that there are no simple answers, no panaceas, no silver bullet solutions for this complex Continent. Despite the massive influx of assistance from donor countries, non-governmental organizations, charities, international financial institutions, and private foundations, and in spite of the world's leading scholars' devotion and expert analyses, the answers remain elusive while development throughout much of Africa continues to stagnate.

For me, I woke up one day to realize I had long since stopped asking the question. It no longer haunts me.

Instead, I struggle to get through the day-to-day challenges of life in Ethiopia while attempting to provide my children with some semblance of normalcy until we go back to America.

And I am not alone in my yearning to be in the United States. In Ethiopia, the U.S. Embassy's Consular Section is inundated with people requesting to travel to the U.S. for a temporary visit or vacation. Only a small portion of those who request travel visas are approved and a sizeable proportion of those lucky few who receive their visas never return to Ethiopia once reaching America's shores.

During my time in Addis Ababa, newspapers reported that an Ethiopian man was discovered in the cargo bin of an Ethiopian Air jet upon its arrival in Washington, DC. Found wrapped in a shopping bag inside the cargo in the plane's underbelly, he is to have said upon discovery, "I'd rather be in jail in America for this than live in my country." Another anecdote involves a friend that took her Ethiopian nanny with her to the U.S. for a three-week vacation. The nanny disappeared after one week. She simply took the trash out one morning and never came back, choosing an illegal life in the U.S. over returning to her home in Addis Ababa.

But many of the Ethiopians who end up immigrating to the U.S. do so legally, acquiring their U.S. tourist visas in advance and then applying for political asylum immediately upon touching down in America. Many of these asylum claims, I'm told by Ethiopian friends, are based on fabricated stories, with savvy U.S. immigration lawyers coaching their clients on what to say and how to say it so as to elicit maximum sympathy from the adjudicating American judges.

This transplant asylum life in America, however, while seemingly the holy grail solution for many Ethiopians dreaming of a better life, is not always what it's cracked up to be. For some of these immigrants, they find themselves crippled by nostalgia as they long for their homeland. For the intensely proud Ethiopian - hailing from the cradle of humanity, an independent nation that evaded being colonized, and a land renowned for its unique music, dance, and culinary traditions virtually untouched by outside influences for centuries - it can be surprisingly daunting to adjust to life in America; a place that seems to be obsessed with material excess and lacking a distinctive identity, drowning in its own sea of diversity.

Mesfin once described one such Ethiopian asylum friend to me, a man now living in Maryland and working as an accountant. Visiting this affluent Ethiopia-American friend in his city apartment one day, this asylum friend admitted to Mesfin that, despite the material good life he has carved out for himself after gaining legal asylum status in America, he is depressed and disappointed in life. His good fortune and considerable advantages aside, by consequence of his political asylum status (apparently granted based on a fabricated story that left his "gullible and naive" judge in tears), this man is forever banned from returning to his country; a land he longs to see, to one day again feel. Ethiopia's rhythms beat in his heart and remain deeply ingrained in his soul, but, legally unable to quench this thirst for his country, he is left parched and pining for his homeland while living out his days in Maryland.

At this point, you may ask, why did he do it – if he loves his country so deeply, why did leave? His answer, as is the answer of so many other adult immigrants lost in the memories of their homeland, is that he did it for his children, so that they may grow up in a land that can deliver a promising future. He did it so that his children won't know fear – fear of arbitrarily losing everything that the family created in one capricious sweep emanating from a government, a rebel group, or some other band of criminals. Ultimately, he, like the multitude of other immigrants drawn to America, selflessly sacrificed his happiness for the hopes, the future, and the promise of his children.

And people keep coming to the U.S., despite our prevailing politics, despite our missteps and mistakes in the world, because we continue to deliver on that promise to our children. My own progression in life is testament to this sentiment. Coming from inauspicious beginnings, born into a typical middle class family with no significant political or social connections to speak of and a mediocre academic record at best, I managed to achieve my dream to join the U.S. Foreign Service and now proudly serve my country overseas as a diplomat. I accomplished this through hard work, dedication, and perseverance. With the unflappable support of loving parents, I was able to succeed because I live in a land of opportunity; a country founded on the premise of equality and firmly grounded in its commitment to meritocracy.

In practical terms, this means that a basketball-skipping, fashion backwards, terrible dancer who can't snap and who spent her summers on Wallyworld cross-country camping adventures has the possibility to perhaps one day reach the rank of U.S. Ambassador.

In more theoretical terms, it means that in this land of meritocracy and opportunity, to hope is not audacious. We often resort to hope in the face of adversity, because we come from a place where hope, tenacity, and talent can be enough to effect positive change and achieve dreams. But for the competent, hard-working, dedicated Africans who remain in their countries with the goal of making their continent a better place, the harsh reality is that to hope can, in fact, be audacious. For the educated, middle class Ethiopians who lack political connections and are not members of the ruling elite tribe, to hope is most certainly audacious. For the faceless masses left wallowing in abject poverty, hope is an unknown concept that is out of their reach as they are locked in a perpetual struggle for survival.

It is for all these people that the U.S. serves as a beacon; it provides hope and inspiration to those seeking better ideals and an example of a better way of life. America's strength, as so many prominent politicians, historians, and sociologists have asserted, lies in our willingness to embrace diversity, to respect the individual; in our commitment to America's enduring values that all are equal, all are free, and all deserve a chance to pursue their full measure of happiness.

The U.S. is a place where the son of a man who grew up herding goats in a small, remote Kenyan village can become the President of the United States, with the world looking on in jubilation. And President Obama uses his story to amplify the meaning of America to the world, to pay homage to the land that offers so much, recognizing that "My story is part of the larger American story, that I owe a debt to all of those who came before me, and that in no other country on Earth is my story even possible."

I believe America won't squander the "flowers of support" the world has again spontaneously bestowed upon our threshold in the wake of the historic 2009 American Presidential election. We are a country that hopes, dreams, delivers, and succeeds. We will continue to search for solutions to the world's complex problems, in

Africa and elsewhere. While some may view us as gullible and naive, I counter with pride that we are a country that breeds and fosters optimism; that, as Americans, we will always strive to make the world a better place. We have to.

And through it all - this three-year, emotional and heart-wrenching journey in Africa where I've been forced to question and re-evaluate my world view, my value system, my motivations, and my purpose - I often take comfort in the knowledge that I'm raising my two little American girls to be citizens of the world.

But, living in Ethiopia, my girls have also been exposed to a darker side of life. It is my hope that exposure to these extreme levels of poverty, even at their young ages, will help to instill them with a sense of gratitude for their blessings, and that the benefits of these experiences to their long-term development will be far reaching. I hope that, through this exposure, they will recognize that despite the manmade barriers that separate worlds, we are all fellow human beings sharing one planet and we all deserve access to happiness. I hope that they will take the best of America and fuse it with the positives found throughout the world, seeking solutions to our ongoing international problems in order to make this world a better, more forgiving, and hospitable place for all.

As I stand in the middle of my lush garden in Ethiopia, in the twilight of today's farewell party, in the shadow of my large home that is surrounded by a massive security wall, I say my goodbyes to this handful of souls who have touched my life, to these special people whose stories have changed me from within. I look upon this group of Ethiopians dancing in my yard to their unique rhythmic Ethiopian music with jerking shoulders and fast-rolling head movements, with gratitude and a certain sadness. In their insecure world, they toil without modern conveniences, they are often without electricity or running water, they live in cramped dwellings, and they may be only a step away from answering a dreaded knock at the door or an untimely death from something as innocuous as appendicitis. But still, somehow, they smile.

"Madame. You come," Fasika and Tigist demand with mischievous grins, beckoning me to join their circle and dance. "You looking too sad. You must dance."

"No, no. I'm happy to watch." But before I can finish my short plea for mercy, I am being dragged to the center of their circle. There is no point in arguing with a proud and stubborn Ethiopian, let alone a group of them.

Submitting to the inevitable, I surrender and begin my hideous interpretation of their body jerks and head swirls, making an absolute mockery of their cultural dance to the sound of their uncontrolled laughter.

These are the people that have touched my life, these past three years, with their stories, their strength, their massive potential, their personal struggles, and their small victories. They are people with spirits that will not be suppressed under the fearful, crushing weight of repression and poverty. Somehow, they find a way to carry on, to dance and rejoice in their culture, in life.

But after three years living in their world, in spite of all my luxuries and advantages, I'm tired. After a mere three years here, I find that I have come full circle. Strangely, I now long to live in a cookie cutter two-story brick home with a white picket fence for the family dog, drive the kids to and from sports practice in the family SUV, enroll them in piano lessons, and so on.

I want to live where I have a history. I want to live in the place where people know me inside and out, and where I know them. I want to live where I'm enveloped in a protective embrace, where everything is safe and known because I belong.

I want to be free to hope. I need to smile again. I want to go home. Finally, after a lifetime of searching, Ethiopia has led me home.

EPILOGUE

Home – Are We There Yet?

"....We remain more than a collection of red states and blue states. We are and forever will be the United States of America." – Barak Obama

Lauren, Alexandra, Brian, and I are on the Dulles airport car rental shuttle bus on our way to the Thrifty parking lot, our first moment to relax after leaving

Ethiopia and landing in Virginia. As the bus pulls away from the airport curb and we begin driving along the side roads, my girls both stare intently out the windows in silence. Suddenly, Lauren blurts out, "Wow mommy, this America is a really clean place!"

The other passengers on the bus turn to stare at us with puzzled expressions. Then Alexandra points to a parking area behind a fence full of small planes (personal jets). I tell her those little planes are for the rich, fancy, important people and she replies, "oh, you mean like us in Kenya?" (We had just splurged on a high-end, four-day safari in Kenya's famous Masai Mara before leaving Ethiopia, taking a small propeller plane from Nairobi to the Serengeti plains). This second comment draws in more quizzical looks from the others sharing our Thrifty shuttle bus.

The shuttle finally pulls into the car rental office's parking lot, allowing the bus passengers to file off to get their cars. We are led to a bright blue economy Ford Focus, we put the key in the ignition, roll down all the windows, turn up the radio, and hit the open road for the last leg of our trip – the 1.5 hour drive to my parent's house on the Chesapeake Bay. The radio is blasting the latest upbeat top 40 tunes while the wind whips through my hair for the first time in years. The sense of freedom and open space is exhilarating as I feel the deep layers of

Ethiopia's burdens beginning to peel off, leaving me lighter, happier, freer.

Lost in my own little world of bliss, I look back at Lauren and Alexandra in the car's rear view mirror. Exhausted from our 18 hour or so trip, Alexandra is sound asleep. Lauren is hanging on, operating apparently on adrenaline. In fact, she has a smile from ear to ear as she tilts her face toward the window for maximum wind exposure, like an exuberant puppy on its first car ride. Seeing that I'm looking at her, Lauren turns her head away from the window to look at me and says "this has been a really long journey, mom. Are we there yet?"

Lauren's comment was literal – she was referring to our trip, leaving Ethiopia around midnight, stopping in Khartoum, Sudan to refuel and pick up more passengers, transferring in Amsterdam with a five hour layover, spending another seven hours flying across the Atlantic, and then starting the 1.5 hour drive on the highway. And she wanted to know if we were almost to Grandma and Grandpa's house. I knew this, but her words were strikingly prescient, and they hung heavily in the air. In fact, there was no better comment at the moment and I found myself fighting back repressed tears of relief.

Yes, it had been a very long journey. And yes, Lauren, we are there. We are home.

౭౦౭౦౪౪

Note: The content of this book is based on true stories, although I have taken some creative liberties. Names have been changed to protect privacy. While all of the stories presented are true and recounted to the best of my memory or the memory of the person who disclosed their story to me, some of them have been mixed with and/or attributed to other people. For example, the description of my gardener's home is actually the home of my nanny's sister and my plastic bottle garbage was discovered in the home of a nanny that temporarily worked for me for a few months when I first arrived in Ethiopia. This same nanny was the person who had adopted a little girl from the countryside, not my housekeeper. The appendicitis story happened to the driver of a friend, with my friend being the one to insist that he have the simple, life-saving operation. My husband did not hit a little boy on the Ring Road. Rather, it was a friend and his family of four on their way to a preschool birthday party that had the ring road accident.

The story of a Tesfaye, while an actual person and the discussion described is an approximate summation of our meeting, is more broadly meant to represent the multitude of tireless, passionate "do-gooders," both Ethiopian and foreign, who somehow proliferate in places like Ethiopia. The conversation with the person I call Ted happened between my husband and the man one random day at the Sheraton pool. While his story made a profound impression upon Brian and me, the truth is that it was a one-time encounter and we never saw him again. The farewell party is an invention created as a vehicle to structure the book, although all the situations presented under the context of the party are based on real experiences that have happened to me and/ or my friends over the course of my nearly three years in Ethiopia. Finally, my nanny highlighted throughout the book is now happy in her marriage. In a conversation we had just before I left Ethiopia, she told me she is lucky. She says that she thanks God her husband is good - he is quiet and he lets her be the boss in the home. He doesn't go out drinking with his friends at night and sometimes he even helps with the dishes. What else could you want in life?

In the time between writing this book and it being published, Ethiopia's Prime Minister Meles Zenawi has died. Ethiopia's future post-Meles remains to be seen, but an Ethiopian taxi driver I recently met in Washington, DC as I headed to the airport to return to Seoul after meetings in Washington did not paint a hopeful picture. As so many Ethiopians had told me while I was living in Addis, the regime changes are just another change to the color of the chalk, while the writing on the wall remains the same and the people continue to suffer.

Made in the USA
Middletown, DE
20 January 2023

22654324R00168